T0083273

Georges Clemenceau

Georges Clemenceau

France

David Robin Watson

First published in Great Britain in 2008 by
Haus Publishing Ltd
26 Cadogan Court
Draycott Avenue
London SW3 3BX
www.hauspublishing.com

A CIP catalogue record for this book
is available from the British Library

ISBN 978-1-905791-60-6

Series design by Susan Buchanan
Typeset in Sabon by MacGuru Ltd
Printed in Dubai by Oriental Press
Maps by Martin Lubikowski, ML Design, London

Contents

'Père-la-Victoire': Clemenceau announces the Armistice in the Chamber of Deputies, 11 November 1918.

Preface and Acknowledgements

Georges Clemenceau, prime minister of France, presided over the Peace Conference from its first to its last day, from 18 January 1919 to the formal endings of proceedings on 21 January 1920, which coincided with the end of his government on 20 January. The British prime minister, Lloyd George, had been reluctant to accept Clemenceau as president, even hoping to hold the conference somewhere other than Paris, in order to avoid the likely consequences. But there proved to be no alternative, and Clemenceau neatly stepped from chairing the Supreme War Council which met in Paris in January 1919 to consider problems about the continuation of the armistices to the presidency of the Supreme Council of the Peace Conference.[1] His assumption of this role seems not to have been agreed, but was accepted tacitly: this lack of transparency was part of the failure to define terms, allowing what was for the first three months referred to as the preliminary conference to become the Peace Conference. The implication, at least as understood by many participants, was that there would be a preliminary conference at which the Allies agreed on the terms to present to the enemy, to be followed by a full Conference, or a Congress, as at Vienna in

1815, in which both sides participated. In fact by the time that the Allies had managed to agree aims among themselves after the Herculean struggles in the Council of Four, in March and April 1919, the term preliminary conference was quietly dropped. The Treaty they had drafted was then presented to the German delegation, which was allowed to respond with written observations, but no further discussion took place. In this sense the German accusation that the Treaty was a 'Diktat' was correct, although the changes that were made in response to their protests were not trivial but involved important concessions on the part of the Allies.

Clemenceau's role was crucial at many stages of the negotiations, but never more so than at the session of 7 May 1919 when he presided over the presentation of the Treaty to the German delegation, headed by the Foreign Minister, Brockdorff-Rantzau. This was a vital moment for many reasons. In the first place it was only then that either the Allied or the German publics, or the German government, became aware of the terms of the Treaty. For the most part the previous Allied negotiations had been kept secret, in spite of some leaks. For all sides sudden revelation of the terms came as a bombshell. But the ceremony was a key moment also for its symbolic impact, and for what it betrayed about the two leading participants. Only Clemenceau and Brockdorff-Rantzau spoke. Clemenceau declared: *The hour has come for the heavy reckoning of accounts. You have asked us for peace; we are disposed to grant it ... I must add that this second peace of Versailles has been too dearly bought by all the peoples represented here for us not to be unanimously resolved to obtain by all the means in our power the legitimate satisfactions which are due to us.*[2]

Count Brockdorff-Rantzau remained seated to deliver his

prepared reply, which began: 'We are under no illusions as to the extent of our defeat and the degree of our powerlessness. We know that the strength of German arms is broken. We know the intensity of the hatred which meets us … and that as the vanquished we shall be made to pay and as the guilty we shall be punished. The demand is made that we shall acknowledge that we alone are guilty of having caused the war. Such a confession in my mouth would be a lie.' He went on to attribute the war to 50 years of imperialism by all European states, and in particular to the 'murderous hands' which had assassinated the heir to the Austrian throne and to Russian mobilisation. Although admitting German war crimes he insisted that both sides were equally guilty of such crimes, and that the Allies had continued them after the armistice by maintaining the blockade of Germany which had caused the death of 'hundreds of thousands of non-combatants, destroyed coolly and deliberately after our opponents had won a certain and assured victory'. He then called on the peace of justice that Germany had been promised according to the principles of President Wilson.[3]

Clemenceau's speech, very brief, courteous but perfectly forthright, left no doubt about the matters that he felt were essential. One word 'second', drew attention to the fact that this treaty was to be signed at Versailles, because the Prussian government in 1871 had chosen Versailles not only to dictate their peace terms to the defeated French, but also to transform Prussia into the German Empire.[4] They had chosen Versailles because it was the palace of Louis XIV; the German Empire thus claimed the hegemony of Europe after defeating the French who had asserted their hegemony in earlier centuries. Clemenceau now spoke not for France alone, but for the Allies as a whole, the *small and great powers who had united to fight the hardest war that had been imposed on them.* His second sentence stressed that the Germans had asked for peace and that the Allies were prepared to grant it.

Brockdorff-Rantzau's reply was much longer: the manner and tone of its delivery produced the most deplorable effect on his audience, especially on President Wilson, and probably accounted for the fact that in the subsequent discussion he was mainly on the side of Clemenceau in resisting Lloyd George's attempts to weaken the terms. Wilson was convinced that the terms presented to the Germans already represented a just, if stern, settlement. Wilson said to Lord Riddell: 'The Germans are really a stupid people … This is the most tactless speech I have ever heard. It will set the whole world against them.' This exchange in the Hôtel Trianon at Versailles can be seen to represent in miniature the subsequent history of the peace settlement. It illustrated the enormous gulf between the attitudes of the two sides. Clemenceau was convinced that France and its allies had fought a war imposed on them by Germany, a war to defend the values of European civilisation threatened by German domination and by the methods of barbarism they had employed. Brockdorff-Rantzau, of course, rejected that view totally. With a strained interpretation of the facts he sought to reverse the Allied accusations about the cause of the war, and about the barbarity of its conduct. His claims were without foundation and represent the victim mentality adopted by Germany from the first moment of the Peace Conference. Brockdorff-Rantzau advised the German government not to sign the Treaty. His advice was rejected, entailing his resignation and the formation of a new government which finally signed, under protest, at the last moment before the expiry of the Allied ultimatum on 24 June 1919. It could be argued that it would have been better for the future of mankind if Germany had made Brockdorff-Rantzau's choice. Refusal to sign would have faced the Allies with the need to occupy and rule Germany with all the dangers of revolution and disorder that that would have entailed. But the German authorities were equally reluctant to face those dangers, and thus signed the Treaty with every intention of resisting its application in any way they could. Thus history unrolled as in a Greek tragedy: there were alternative choices but the historian can see why the alternative roads were not taken, and why the most probable, if not the inevitable route, was the route which was taken.

ooooo

The confrontation between Clemenceau and Brockdorff-Rantzau on 7 May showed that the Treaty would not be accepted by Germany, it would have to be enforced on it by the victors. Detailed examination of the terms and of their gradual adjustment to meet German resistance will allow us to reach a verdict on the Treaty. Was it really 'too weak for its severity'[5] or did it contain within its terms enough to restrain the German attempt to revise it without a repetition of the World War? This book will examine Clemenceau's part in the decision-making from the armistices of October-November 1918 to the signing of the Treaty of Versailles on 28 June 1919; it will then briefly recount his role in the making of the treaties with the other enemy powers, Austria, Hungary, Bulgaria and the Ottoman Empire, and his defence of the Versailles Treaty in the French parliament: finally it will deal with his defence of the Treaty during the last years of his life, ending with the book *Grandeur and Misery of Victory* on which he was still working when he died, at the age of 88 in November 1929.

Acknowledgements

Thanks first of all to Judith, without whose computer skills this book could never have been completed in time. It is in a very real sense a joint effort.

I would also like to express my appreciation to the Musée Clemenceau and the Société des Amis de Clemenceau, to the late Georges and André Wormser, and to Marcel Wormser, who have done so much to help historical study of Clemenceau, and also to keep his memory alive through their personal links with him. I must also record my gratitude to Professor Renouvin who, 40 years ago, guided my first approach to study of this topic. It was an immense privilege to meet this great historian, himself seriously wounded at the Front, who spent his life establishing the truth about the war, its causes and the peace settlement that followed.

Finally, to explain why events which may seem to be in the distant past still have emotional resonance that cannot be disguised, I would like to dedicate this work to the memory of Private Fred Margerison, killed on the Somme, 15 February 1917, aged 21, and to his widow, Sarah Ellen, my mother.

Clemenceau in 1879, painted by Edouard Manet.

I

The Life and the Land

1

France in the World

France was one of the victorious Allied powers in 1918, but it was by then the weakest of the three: in population and industrial development it had been left behind by Britain, still more by the British Empire which was seen in 1918 as far more of a unitary power than it really was, and by the United States. More importantly France was also much smaller and weaker than Germany, and found herself, at least for the immediate future, without the Russian Empire as an ally to hold Germany in check from the east. So the victory of 1918 was fragile. As will be seen throughout this study, it placed Clemenceau in a dilemma. He needed to maintain the tripartite coalition that had defeated Germany, but he could not be sure that his two partners would even in the short term, still less over the future years, remain convinced that their own interests bound them to ally with France. He was convinced, as was the great majority of French opinion, that Germany would not willingly accept a peace settlement acceptable to the Allies: it would have to be defended and enforced. But Woodrow Wilson unequivocally, and Lloyd George equivocally and inconsistently, hoped for German goodwill that would accept a settlement that did not need to be defended by force of arms. Although Clemenceau sought with all his strength to maintain the unity of the victors, and thought that he had attained it, his dilemma was that he also needed to win safeguards for France in case it was left to enforce the Treaty without Anglo-Saxon support, as indeed happened. But the more safeguards he won, the more resentment there was on the German side, and the more firmly held the belief in the United States and Britain that German resentment was the result of French failure to be reasonable.

The background to this situation is that France in 1918 was a fairly long way down the road of decline as a great European power. It is not just that France was weaker than Germany, but that French memories went back over the centuries to when France had herself been by far the most powerful European state, outclassing all others in population, wealth and military strength. In the first half of the 20th century Germany could aspire to conquer the whole of Europe, and almost achieve it in 1941–2, but in earlier times it was France herself who had almost succeeded in putting the whole of Europe under its monarch. One can see a remarkably similar pattern in the two histories. Nazi Germany in the Second World War took the half-unconscious 'Grasping after World Power' by the Wilhelmine Reich of 1914–18 to an even more barbarous and murderous conclusion, achieving far more success in the brief period before Hitler's hubris threw everything away. The same pattern is there in Louis XIV's efforts to dominate Europe, picked up by Napoleon, the sacrifice of even more millions of human lives, and the achievement by the time of the treaties of Tilsit in 1807 of what could have been long-enduring French dominance, thrown away by the Emperor's hubris.

The fundamental factor behind France's decline was demographic. At the time of Louis XIV and Napoleon France was by far the most populous state in Europe. Any potential evolution of the 'Holy Roman Empire of the German Nation' into a German national state had been vetoed by the Thirty Years War (1618–48) and the treaties of Westphalia of 1648. Eighteenth-century France was a demographic giant, surrounded by less populous states. Even in 1850, with a population of 35 million, it still had a higher population than any other European state except Russia, and would even have equalled the population of a united Germany if it had existed. But the loss of Alsace-Lorraine in 1871 brought the German population to 41 million against France's 36 million, and by 1914 Germany had over 65 million to France's 39 million. After the war with the return of Alsace-Lorraine to France and the loss of other pre-war German territories, Germany still had a population of 63 million to France's 39 million. Even more striking was the rise of Germany as an industrial power; by 1914 German coal and steel production were both four times that of France. Thus although the experience of the war showed that France had the strength to resist the German onslaught it was only by making a superhuman effort, by mobilising and losing a higher proportion of its young male population and with the aid of its allies. Because of the lower French birth-rate, itself the long-term cause of the relative decline of the French population, it would be more difficult for France to replace this missing generation.

Although these demographic trends made a comparative decline inevitable, the history of France over the last two centuries has not been one of steady decline. The virtually complete domination of Europe west of the Russian and Turkish empires achieved by Napoleon could never be repeated once the Emperor's overweening ambition had lost it. But the balance of power system in a Europe where for two centuries there were five great powers (Britain, France, Russia, Austria-Hungary and Prussia/Germany) meant that a potential hegemon would eventually be faced by a combined challenge from the others. Thus France recovered from its defeats in 1815 and 1870 and has continued to this day to play its part in the international system.

The story of France as a great power can be seen as a roller-coaster ride from the triumphs of Tilsit in 1807, to defeat at Waterloo in 1815, slow recovery to the point where Napoleon III hosted the peace congress in 1856 to end the Crimean War, a plunge down to defeat at Sedan in 1870, followed by the triumph of victory in 1918, descent to total defeat in 1940, and then the restoration of its status in the post-Second World War world, as a permanent member of the United Nations Security Council and as a state with nuclear weapons. As General de Gaulle put it more poetically in the opening sentences of his War Memoirs: 'The emotional side of me tends to imagine France like the princess in the fairy stories or the Madonna in the frescoes as dedicated to an exceptional and exalted destiny ... Providence has created her either for complete successes or exemplary misfortunes.'[1]

'The emotional side of me tends to imagine France like the princess in the fairy stories or the Madonna in the frescoes as dedicated to an exceptional and exalted destiny ... Providence has created her either for complete successes or exemplary misfortunes.'

GENERAL DE GAULLE

The Congress of Vienna in 1815 constructed a territorial settlement designed to hold France in check, which in the main preserved peace in Europe until Napoleon III established the

Second Empire and began to challenge the Vienna settlement. His small, short wars seemed at first to be successful but it soon emerged that his policies, far from increasing the power and prestige of France, had created the conditions for a united Italy and Germany. The latter was to emerge from the rapid and total defeat of Napoleon's armies in the Franco-Prussian War. As well as losing the provinces of Alsace and Lorraine, and being subjected to occupation by the German army until an indemnity that more than covered the cost of the war had been paid, France was humiliated when the new German Empire was proclaimed in Louis XIV's Palace of Versailles.

At first many people in France dreamed of a war of revenge that would overturn the Treaty of Frankfurt that ended the Franco-Prussian War, but those who ruled knew that such were senseless dreams. As the years went by the imbalance between the French Third Republic and the German Empire became steadily greater. Yet, France was still one of the Great Powers and the possibility of forming a combination that would challenge Germany remained open. The German Chancellor Bismarck was a skilled enough player of the diplomatic game to keep France isolated, managing to weld together the Triple Alliance of Germany, Austria-Hungary and Italy in 1882.

Until his dismissal in 1890 Bismarck also managed to maintain good relations between Germany and Russia, in spite of the underlying conflict between Austria-Hungary and Russia in the Balkans, the very conflict that in the end led to the outbreak of the First World War. Like a skilled juggler he kept these different balls in the air throughout the 1880s, controlling a diplomatic system in which an isolated France could not hope to reverse its defeat. Instead, with Bismarck's encouragement, France built a vast colonial empire overseas, second only to the British Empire in territorial extent and in population. Expansion began in 1881–2 with the protectorate of Tunis, which was added to its existing possessions, Algeria which had been conquered in 1830, and a few footholds in Africa and Indo-China acquired by the Second Empire. Conquest of Indo-China followed in 1884–5. In the next ten years Madagascar was taken, together with a huge expanse of territory in west and central Africa. At the same time other European powers expanded their colonial possessions in 'the scramble for Africa', inspired by the French example.

This colonial policy was the work of the centre group of conservative republicans, in power from 1879 onwards, and was attacked by both the Radical Left and the Monarchist Right. Its exponents were Léon Gambetta and Jules Ferry. Ferry, in particular, argued the economic case for colonies, which in fact turned out to be misguided. The new French colonies were not suitable for settlement by Europeans, and in any case France had no surplus population to people its colonies. France was instead the only major European country to take in immigrants in this period. And although France was second only to Britain as an investor of capital abroad, only a tiny proportion of its capital exports went to the colonies. It seems that the real motives for the acquisition of the French Empire were politico-psychological. For those who supported the policy it was seen as an expression of national vigour and self-confidence; they invoked the 'civilising mission', French equivalent of the 'white man's burden'. Ferry defended his policy in a speech in the Chamber of Deputies of 28 July 1885 in which he declared: 'You cannot hold up before France an ideal that would be suitable for Belgium or Switzerland. France cannot merely be free: she must be great, exercising over the destinies of Europe all the influence which is rightly hers, and carrying it all over the world ... The alternative is a policy of abdication which will in the long run lead to decadence.'[2] Opponents rejected this argument on the grounds that it distracted France from its true task of reversing the defeat of 1870–1. Paul Déroulède, leader of the League of Patriots, said that France must reject the bargain by which 20 negro maidservants were offered in exchange for its two daughters, that is, the provinces of Alsace and Lorraine. Clemenceau campaigned against overseas adventures from 1881 to 1885: his intervention meant that France withdrew from a joint invasion of Egypt in 1882, leaving Britain to establish informal control there that lasted over 60 years: in 1885 he brought down Ferry's government over Indo-China but did not reverse the conquest of that area.

Even before Bismarck's fall from power in 1890 the contradictions of his alliance system were appearing, even if contained. The basic problem was the potential rivalry between Germany's closest ally, Austria-Hungary and Russia if the 'sick man of Europe', the Ottoman Empire, finally collapsed. Everyone could foresee this eventuality long before it happened. Russian rivalry with Austria-Hungary in the Balkans made a rapprochement between the Tsarist Empire and France an obvious step. It began with French financial moves into Russia, beginning from about 1887. Over the next five years the inner circles of the political establishment were aware of the growing sympathy between France and Russia. One of the few opponents was Clemenceau whose dream was an alliance, or at least an understanding with England; he saw this pair as the only two of the Great Powers who were really progressive and liberal, and at this stage of his life dreamed of their ideological partnership, rather than an alliance with reactionary Tsarist Russia, based on *realpolitik*. He had talked of this Anglo-French partnership with the two

Radicals Joseph Chamberlain and Morley in the 1880s, and again with Joseph Chamberlain in 1891.[3]

Chamberlain's radicalism turned into imperialism, and in the 1890s he became intensely Francophobic. In any case, in view of Lord Salisbury's reluctance to indulge the French in this way, an Anglo-French alliance was impossible. Instead France and Russia came together in an entente of 1891, and a military convention of August 1892 finally ratified by the two parties on 27 December 1893 and 4 January 1894. The Franco-Russian alliance matched the Triple Alliance of Germany, Austria-Hungary and Italy in a pattern that lasted until the outbreak of war in 1914. As the alliances lasted for over 20 years of peace, it cannot be argued, as it once was by opponents of the 'old diplomacy', that they inevitably meant war. Some of the elements of the confrontation between the great powers that were to lead to the First World War were in place. But in the short term France's increased self-confidence was expressed mainly in steps overseas that led to bad-tempered exchanges with Britain over West Africa and Siam. The really important point for France, however, was to prevent Britain from turning its informal rule in Egypt into something that was virtually a protectorate. The complicated international arrangements about the Egyptian debt seemed to offer an opportunity that could be exploited if France was skilful enough in its diplomatic and naval-military arrangements. The *Jeune École* (young school) of naval strategists developed a fleet that it was hoped would be, if not an outright challenge to the British

'A dream came before his [Chamberlain's] vision as we sauntered down the boulevard, a dream of practical co-operation with Clemenceau in the common interest of European democracy.'
VISCOUNT MORLEY[4]

fleet, at least a thorn in its flesh; a sort of miniature version of the Tirpitz 'risk theory'. Meanwhile the French penetrated eastwards from Senegal along the semi-desert southern fringe of the Sahara. At their most optimistic, French colonialists dreamed of eventually linking this up through the Sudan to Ethiopia and Djibouti, their Red Sea foothold in Somaliland. The result was the Fashoda crisis, which at least in the eyes of the general public in the two countries brought Britain and France to the brink of war. Colonel Marchand, despatched years earlier at the head of 200 Senegalese troops reached Fashoda on the upper reaches of the White Nile in July 1898. Almost simultaneously Kitchener's forces advancing south from Egypt re-established British control of the Sudan, after the Mahdist revolt. French ideas of an east-west block of African territory from Senegal to Somaliland were shown to be an illusion. Access to the Upper Nile, difficult enough in any case, was only really possible from Egypt. On a wider scale the French government was forced to recognise the huge disparity of naval strength between France and Britain: there was, of course, no question of Russian help against Britain. France simply had to accept that 1882 had been decisive, and that British control of Egypt was unchallengeable.

These events illustrate a basic dilemma with which France was confronted from its geographical position. Its long coastlines tempted France to become a maritime and colonial power, with interests throughout the overseas world, as had already happened in the early modern period. Yet the vulnerable north-eastern frontier, so open and so close to Paris, and centuries of historical tradition, compelled it also to intervene in the land wars of the European continent. Great colonial empires could be acquired and preserved by even minor powers on the fringes of the continent, Portugal,

Spain, Holland, even Belgium, and also of course, by Britain, protected by the Channel. But France was torn between two destinies. Continental dangers and ambitions led to the loss of the major part of its first overseas empire by the end of the 18th century. The acquisition of a second empire overseas between 1870 and 1912, looked far more impressive on global maps than it proved to be in reality. Intended by Bismarck to bring France and Britain into permanent conflict with each other, after Fashoda France realised that its colonial empire depended on remaining on good terms with Britain. Nothing else was possible as long as the military threat from Germany loomed so obviously over the plains to the north and east of Paris. Théophile Delcassé, the new foreign minister, abandoned his previous ideas and sought instead to win compensation for abjuring French awkwardness in Egypt. Thus the basis was laid for the bargain that made the Entente Cordiale of 1904: France gave Britain a free hand in Egypt while Britain agreed not to oppose French attempts to gain control of Morocco.

Although the Entente Cordiale was a settling of past differences and not intended to be an alliance, Germany's reaction virtually turned it into one. The place of Morocco in the diplomacy of the years 1905–12 is that it became a bargaining chip and a symbol of the relations between the Great Powers. Germany did not want Morocco for herself, but wanted to force France to realise that the price to be paid for absorption of Morocco into its North African sphere was breaking off the Entente with Britain. Their reaction to what was seen as aggressive German bullying, combined with the German naval building, brought Britain and France closer together. These diplomatic realignments took place first in the Conference of Algeçiras of 1906 at which all the powers met to discuss the future of Morocco. The military strength of the Triple Alliance against the Franco-Russian alliance was at this moment at its highest point, as Russia's defeat by Japan was followed by the revolutionary disturbances of 1905–6. As for France, army morale had been weakened by the aftermath of the Dreyfus Affair (see Chapter 2), and effectives reduced by the conscription law of 1905, reducing service to two years. But neither side envisaged immediate war in 1906, and Germany was diplomatically isolated. The conference did not give France a free hand in Morocco but at least it gave it a privileged position, which it continued to exploit in the next five years. Equally important was the fact that on 31 January 1906 Sir Edward Grey, Foreign Secretary in the new Liberal government, authorised talks between the British and French general staffs about their co-operation in the face of a German invasion of France. The Franco-British Entente was not an alliance, and Grey could claim that he had left his hands free, but there was a sense in which these military talks involved as much of a commitment as an alliance. As the French could ask in 1914, when the German invasion came, if Britain did not join them, what would have happened to the word 'honour' in the English language.

Shortly after the Algeçiras conference Clemenceau formed his first government, being prime minister from October 1906 to July 1909. Whereas previous foreign ministers had enjoyed considerable independence, with premiers and cabinets who took little interest in foreign affairs, this was no longer the case. Clemenceau's foreign minister was Stephen Pichon who had long been his protégé. Throughout his long career as a diplomat, administrator and politician, Pichon was always seen as an able executant rather than an independent decision maker, and as Clemenceau's lieutenant. That was especially so in his two periods as Clemenceau's foreign minister, 1906–9 and 1917–20.

France's relationship with Germany was the main problem in its foreign policy. Clemenceau believed that war would come in the long run, and wrote in a letter to his Danish friend Brandes in 1906: *No, my friend, Germany will not declare war on us [at this moment]. But in my opinion the European situation is such that a great armed conflict is inevitable at some time which I cannot foresee, and our duty is to prepare for the worst.* To the French diplomat Georges Louis he said in July 1908: *I think war is inevitable. We must do nothing to provoke it, but we must be ready for it; helped by Russia and England, doubtless by Spain also and perhaps by Italy as well, we may be able to win. In any case it will be a life and death affair; if we are beaten we will be crushed.*[5]

The impulsiveness of the Kaiser rather than a planned German attack was what he feared, but Clemenceau's policy was neither hostile nor provocative. He was accused by left-wing revisionists of hostility and chauvinism, but it is hard to see how this judgement is justified. His public statements were firm rather than chauvinistic, and his government pursued good working relations with Germany. While he was in power France and Germany did not quarrel over Morocco. Germany held the military balance; Britain was nowhere near becoming a European military power, and Russia would need years to recover from its defeat by Japan. So Clemenceau had very good reasons for postponing the inevitable war as long as possible. Until there were major military commitments from Britain and from Russia, two of his major concerns, it was vital that France kept on reasonable but dignified terms with Germany. He also had to deal with the powerful pacifist and anti-militarist feelings held by many of his own Radical party as well as the Socialists. If war came it was very important that it should be seen to be the consequence of intolerable provocation of the part of the Germans, and not on some obscure issue. In the first months of the Clemenceau government the most important development was the Anglo-Russian entente in August 1907, concerning the delimitation of British and Russian interests in Persia, Tibet and Afghanistan: French involvement in these was limited to general expressions of approval. France played a more active diplomatic role in attempting to improve on the Anglo-military conversations of 1906 by securing a commitment to a larger British army ready for intervention if needed on the Continent. Clemenceau was concerned that the tendency seemed to be towards a reduction of such a commitment.

When the British prime minister Sir Henry Campbell-Bannerman visited Paris in 1907, Clemenceau tried to raise the army question, and was disconcerted when Campbell-Bannerman said that he did not think that public opinion would allow British troops to be employed on the Continent. Later his ambassador said that Clemenceau had misunderstood the position: a British army would under no circumstances be sent to fight on the Continent. Clemenceau was still concerned at the disparity between the strength of France's diplomatic position and the weakness of the military force of the Entente Powers. In 1908 he tried several times to emphasise this concern to the British government. At a meeting with Grey in April 1908, 'he dwelt with great emphasis upon the certainty that we should have to intervene on the Continent of Europe against any power which attained a position of domination there just as we had to do in the time of Napoleon. He said that we ought to be prepared for this'.[6]

Clemenceau followed this conversation by encouraging the

writing of a series of newspaper articles pointing out that France was endangered and demanding a stronger British army, and later in the year in meetings, which included King Edward VII at lunch in the spa town of Carlsbad. He was reported as speaking with the force and speed of an express train for nearly two hours, again emphasising the extreme danger for France until Britain developed a bigger and more effective army. Asquith, the new British prime minister, was annoyed at this, writing that the French premier's ignorance was great if he thought that the British were going to keep a large army ready to meet the Germans on the Continent. French attempts at that time to get Russian military commitments were equally unsuccessful. They could not count on Russian help in the event of war.

But the main reason for seeking a settlement in Morocco by both France and Germany was caused by the Austrian annexation of Bosnia in October 1908, which led to deterioration of relations between Austria and Russia, causing both France and Germany to seek to mend relations. In January 1909 Germany proposed an agreement with France on Morocco, as a restraining influence. It was not so significant in its impact on Morocco as in its implications for the European diplomatic system, part of a general Franco-German rapprochement, which continued in various ways for the next 12 months. At the time it was viewed by the British ambassador to Russia as the beginning of a collapse in Anglo-French-Russian understanding, with the danger that England would be isolated. The French attitude in the Bosnian crisis, together with the agreement on Morocco, showed that they were unreliable partners. Clemenceau's main concern was no doubt the fact that France felt exposed, as a result of Russia's weakness and unreliability, along with the British refusal to enlarge its army so it could be used in the event of a war on the Continent. The danger of the whole situation had been highlighted by the Bosnian crisis, over which Clemenceau had no intention of becoming involved in a war with Germany.[7]

Clemenceau fell from power in July 1909 but remained an influential figure in the French parliament. He played a major role in the next international crisis in the summer of 1911, when the Germans sent a gunboat to Agadir, in response to French troops moving into the Moroccan capital Fez. The German government saw this as a breach both of the Algeçiras convention and the Franco-German agreement on Morocco. In 1911 the danger of the crisis escalating into war was far greater than it had been in 1905–6. Nonetheless it was avoided and produced an agreement by which France at last got a free hand to turn Morocco into a protectorate in return for ceding territory in central Africa to Germany. This was certainly not a bad bargain for France. It was the work of the prime minister, Joseph Caillaux, who had been finance minister in Clemenceau's first government. The foreign minister, de Selves, was inexperienced, and Caillaux thought that he was in danger of being pushed into reckless acts by anti-German permanent officials in the Quai d'Orsay. So he took the conduct of negotiations into his own hands by using unofficial channels to Berlin, with the aim of achieving a settlement that would be the basis for developing better relations with Germany over the long term. This was anathema to Clemenceau who was determined to bring down Caillaux's government. He was able to do this in January 1912 by exploiting contradictory statements by the prime minister and his foreign minister about the conduct of the negotiations. Caillaux fell and was replaced as prime minister by Raymond Poincaré, a change that was a decisive step towards what has been seen as a national revival in France. The treaty with Germany was ratified and although it favoured France, in the changed atmosphere was almost seen as a defeat. Poincaré, as prime minister and then President from 1913, dominated French foreign policy until the outbreak of war. The causes of the First World War, a subject that has produced an astronomical amount of historical writing, cannot be analysed here, although they will be mentioned later in discussion of the war guilt clauses of the Treaty.[8]

A rational calculation of the relative strength of the two sides that went to war in 1914 would have shown the probability of German defeat. A combination of Russia, France and Britain outclassed Germany and Austria-Hungary in manpower and industrial capacity. In the long run the Allies would win if they continued united in the struggle, which was precisely why Germany launched what it hoped would be a short, decisive war. Britain's potential capacity for land warfare in Europe was discounted by the German authorities, and their strategy was to knock out France in a few weeks, as in 1870, and then to deal with Russia. This plan had failed by October 1914, when the Battle of the Marne checked the German invasion and the front line settled across northern France in a position that did not change much until August 1918. In 1915 the Central

Advocates of a 'new diplomacy' in 1919 and after attacked the 'secret treaties' of pre-1914. In fact, although the terms of the treaties were, in theory, secret, there was nothing secret about the existence of the treaties and the alignment of the powers they represented. Germany, Austria-Hungary and Italy had been allied since 1882, although Italy did not support the central powers in 1914. The Franco-Russian alliance was made in 1893–4, while Britain signed ententes, not alliances, with France in 1904 and Russia in 1907. Although the immediate cause of the war was Russian support for Serbia in the face of the ultimatum from Austria-Hungary, Serbia and Russia were not bound by a treaty of alliance.

Powers were able to advance hundreds of miles eastwards, but in essence the situation on the Eastern Front was the same. The German-Austrian armies had conquered territory but they had not broken their opponent's military capacity. Thus the stalemate, with its terrible slaughter of men on both sides, continued until 1916 in the East and the summer of 1918 in the West. The problem was that Germany would not relinquish the territorial gains it had made in the first two months of the war, while the Allies were equally determined to reverse them, to achieve a victory that would protect them from a repetition of the 1914 attack. Neither side would accept the *status quo* of 1914. Down to August 1918, the German authorities would only contemplate a settlement in which they kept the strategically important areas won from France and Belgium, and the much larger empire won from Russia in the East. On the other hand, the rulers of Britain and France were convinced that they had the strength to push Germany back if they continued to fight. As they were liberal countries their governments were challenged by some who wished to make peace, but they never came near to winning control of policy in either Britain or France. In any case advocates of a compromise peace were completely deluded about what the German terms would have been. In 1916 Lloyd George replaced Asquith as British prime minister in a new coalition, including a strong conservative element determined to win the war. In France political combinations were more complex, but under the governments of Briand, Alexandre Ribot and Paul Painlevé, the same determination was maintained. Only in Russia did the February 1917 revolution eventually bring to power in November of that year a Bolshevik government, financed by the Germans, and prepared to seek peace. It was at this point that Clemenceau returned to power as prime minister of France.

2

Clemenceau in French Politics

Clemenceau has often been depicted in Anglo-Saxon accounts as cynical and reactionary.[1] The most famous such characterisation was the pen portrait made by J M Keynes in *The Economic Consequences of the Peace*, a pamphlet as misjudged as it was successful, and as disastrous in its influence as it was well-written. Clemenceau's political position in 1919 was not on the Right, although he was supported by the Right, as well as by the Centre and the non-Socialist left.

'... throned, in his grey gloves, on the brocade chair, dry in soul and empty of hope, very old and tired, but surveying the scene with a cynical and almost impish air.'
KEYNES ON CLEMENCEAU, PRESIDING AT ONE OF THE MEETINGS OF THE CONFERENCE.[2]

Clemenceau was never right-wing, still less reactionary, in French political terms. The division between left and right began in France at the time of the Revolution of 1789, from where the terms and the concepts spread, and became current usage throughout Europe and the world. To be on the Right in France meant to be against the Revolution, to be on the Left to be in favour of it. No one insisted on this more strongly than Clemenceau himself, who had in 1891 coined the phrase *the Revolution is a Bloc*, meaning that it had to be accepted or rejected as a whole. The Revolution came into conflict with the Catholic Church in a nation whose population was predominantly Catholic. This conflict was the central fact of French political history during Clemenceau's lifetime. The Right defended the claims of the Catholic Church, while the Left fought for and achieved between 1902 and 1905 a secular state, seen by them as neutral in religious matters, but attacked by the Right as being inimical to the Catholic religion. Although not himself in office at the time of the separation of Church and State in 1905 Clemenceau was without doubt one of the most influential figures in the campaigns that moved from defence of Dreyfus to the establishment of a secular republic, achieving something that had been on the republican programme since 1870.

Certainly Clemenceau was never a revolutionary, nor a Marxist or collectivist Socialist. His political stance was exemplified in the title of the party that was the main element in his two governments, of 1906–9 and 1917–20, the Parti Républicain Radical et Radical-Socialiste, although paradoxically he was never a leading member of that party. What this means is that at the beginning of his political life he was on the extreme left of non-revolutionary politics, but that as the years went by he came to be on the Centre Left. For by the time he formed his first government in 1906, the Radical-Socialists were outflanked on their left by the collectivist socialists who had united under the title of Section Française de l'Internationale Ouvrière (SFIO: French Section of the Workers' International). While this SFIO claimed to be revolutionary and Marxist, it soon became clear that in great majority it was neither. Nevertheless it was this development that allowed Clemenceau to be portrayed misleadingly as right-wing by the time of his second government. Another reason for this false perspective is the shift in the respective attitudes of Left and Right on patriotism and war. At the time of the Revolution a patriot was a revolutionary, and nothing had changed when Clemenceau's political life began. During the Franco-Prussian War and the Paris Commune of 1871, the Left were the advocates of continued resistance, while the Right wanted peace. By the turn of the century, and for one reason among several, because of the Dreyfus Affair these attitudes had been reversed. In the years before 1914 the Right had warned of the danger from Germany while the SFIO had preached conciliation, dreaming that the Socialist International could prevent war. Thus Clemenceau's determination to overthrow defeatism, and to continue the war until victory was won, made him anathema to the Left. But this was an attitude that developed at the time of his second ministry, when the SFIO began to move away from the support for the war that it had embraced in the Sacred Union of 1914. Thus in order to understand Clemenceau's position in French political life it is necessary to examine his whole political career from its beginning during the Second Empire. It can then be seen how Père-la-Victoire (Old Man Victory) could inspire the great majority of the French people with his own willpower and resolution in the final year of the war. His patriotism won over the Right, even the most reactionary of the Royalists, while his impeccable Republican credentials ensured the support of the great majority of the Centre and Left, allowing him for a brief moment to inspire the whole of the French nation.

Clemenceau's political career began 56 years before 1918. In 1862, aged 20 and a medical student, he organised a demonstration against the Second Empire, for which he served a three-month prison sentence. His firm republicanism was inherited from his father, who had himself been briefly imprisoned on political grounds in 1858. He recalled in old age that his father had *made a cult of the Revolution; there were portraits of St Just and Robespierre and others of their kind in every corner of L'Aubraie.*[3]

L'Aubraie was the family house acquired by Clemenceau's great-grandfather at the end of the 18th century, inherited by his father in 1860, and still in the possession of a branch of the family today. It was a fortified manor house, several centuries old, surrounded by a moat and attached to farm buildings; although called the Château de l'Aubraie it was not really as grand as that title would imply. Certainly in Clemenceau's time modern comforts were lacking. It has stone-flagged floors, massive oak beams and vast rooms impossible to heat in winter. It is situated in the Vendée, one of the most isolated, rural and poor areas of France, to the south of Nantes at the mouth of the river Loire. Relations between the Clemenceau family and their peasant tenants were in the patriarchal tradition. Clemenceau's daughter, who spent much of her childhood there wrote: 'Whereas we used the familiar form "tu" to all the village, everyone used the respectful "vous" to us ... In practice one could not have had a more aristocratic education, in spite of the most republican principles.'[4]

Clemenceau's ancestors, who have been traced back to the 16th century, were not aristocrats. They belonged to the middle class of lawyers, doctors, bailiffs and Protestant pastors who gradually accumulated enough wealth to live from their rents as landowners. The family had been Protestant but reverted to a formal adherence to the Catholic religion after the revocation of the Edict of Nantes in 1685. There is surely a connection between this earlier Protestant background and the revolutionary anti-Catholic position they adopted after 1789. Clemenceau's mother, on the other hand, was a practising Protestant. In spite of his atheism and anticlericalism Clemenceau's early upbringing had given him a sound knowledge of the Bible. The Vendée was a region where the Revolution brought outright civil war. Although in great majority fervently Catholic and anti-Revolutionary, there was a minority who supported the Revolution with equal fervour; among this minority are to be found Clemenceau's ancestors. His father, grandfather and great-grandfather, renewing earlier family tradition, all qualified as doctors, but they do not seem to have exercised their profession. They were landowners, not country doctors, and saw a medical degree as an education in natural science, not as training for a job. Clemenceau himself only practised briefly in his early life, without ever seeing it as providing a serious income. He gained his medical degree in Paris in 1865, and soon afterwards departed for the United States, where he spent most of the next three years, mainly in New York. The reason for this emigration seems to have been partly personal, partly political. The personal element was his rejection as a suitor by the family of Hortense Kestner, the young woman he wished to marry. The political reason was his root and branch opposition to the Second Empire. He wanted to study republicanism in operation, in the only major state that was not a monarchy. He also wanted to learn the English language, something he achieved thoroughly by his stay in the United States, and by translating some of John Stuart Mill's works into French. On this basis, developed by his marriage to an American bride who at first knew little French, he came to have a fluent command of English. This was to be important in the negotiations of 1918–19 as neither

Woodrow Wilson nor Lloyd George spoke any French. His marriage ended in divorce in 1892, after which he never remarried, but that still meant that for 23 years he had an Anglophone spouse. He also had many English friends, especially the Maxse family with whom he was intimate over two generations. It can safely be said that Clemenceau was the most Anglophile statesman ever to have occupied a leading position in French politics.

Although at one point he seems to have thought of settling permanently in the United States he changed his mind, perhaps under pressure from his father on whom he was financially dependent, returning to France in June 1868. He had already met the orphaned Mary Plummer who was a pupil at a school where he was employed to teach French, but his proposal had been rejected by her guardian. In November 1868 he heard that the guardian had relented and at the same moment Hortense Kestner announced her engagement to his friend Charles Floquet. He crossed the Atlantic four times over the next seven months, marrying Mary at a civil ceremony in New York on 23 June 1869, before bringing his bride to live with his parents in the Vendée. She stayed there while their three children were born between 1870 and 1873, but her husband left for Paris soon after the outbreak of the Franco-Prussian War.

The Emperor, re-enacting the role of the real Napoleon, took the field with his army, and thus was captured when a large part of it surrendered at Sedan. Little more than a month's fighting had effectively eliminated the French army, thought to be the strongest in Europe. The news reached Paris on 4 September 1870, when the Third Republic was proclaimed in the manner that had by now become a tradition, from the Paris town hall, by a group of republicans without any resistance from the erstwhile authorities. Among the self-appointed group that had seized power were several friends of Clemenceau's father. The young doctor was given a fairly low-level post as mayor of Montmartre, one of 20 districts into which the city of Paris was divided. It turned out however, a few months later, to be a crucial post.

Clemenceau and the republicans had opposed the war while it was being conducted by the Empire, but they now tried to rescue France by a patriotic resurgence of volunteer armies. They called their new regime the Government of National Defence. The original intention to hold almost immediate elections to confirm their authority had to be cancelled in view of the continuing advance of the Prussian army. By 23 September the Prussians had encircled Paris and the government and city were besieged. Léon Gambetta, youngest and most energetic member of the government, escaped from Paris by balloon to establish a delegation at Tours, beyond the reach of the Prussian advance. From there he organised the creation of volunteer armies which attacked the Prussians in vain over the next four months. Meanwhile in Paris the majority of the male population formed itself voluntarily or by conscription into the National Guard. The division between the government in Paris and the delegation in Tours was a fatal error, which allowed the development of a fanatical revolutionary atmosphere in the city. Attempts to break the siege proved futile. By the end of January 1871 the population of Paris was on the verge of starvation and the government was forced to ask Bismarck for an armistice. His terms involved the immediate election of a National Assembly as he refused to make peace with the self-appointed Government of National Defence. They also declared that the French regular army should be demobilised. The National Assembly turned out to have a large monarchist majority as they alone stood for peace while the republicans had been discredited by the failed attempt to continue the war. However Paris and other large cities voted for the republic; it was rural France that rejected it. The Assembly appointed Adolphe Thiers, an Orleanist monarchist, head of the executive power, indicating their rejection of the republic proclaimed in September. His first task was to negotiate terms of peace. They were draconian, loss of the provinces of Alsace and Lorraine, a huge financial indemnity and a triumphal march through Paris.

The leaders of the Paris National Guard were appalled at such humiliating terms. On the pretext of safeguarding 250 cannon the National Guard placed them on the hill of Montmartre in Clemenceau's municipality. Thiers, who had now brought the government back to Paris, decided that they could not be left in the control of the National Guard. On 18 March a small regular army detachment was sent to seize the guns. It met with popular resistance, and the troops mutinied, imprisoning their officers. Clemenceau, having been alerted to their plight, sought to intervene, but too late. Two generals had been slaughtered, in appallingly bloodthirsty scenes. This formed a catalyst by which the whole city revolted and Thiers withdrew to Versailles. The leaders of the National Guard proclaimed elections for a revolutionary Commune, copied from that of 1792. Clemenceau and some other municipal mayors attempted to mediate between the National Guard and the National Assembly and Thiers. Their plan was to organise elections with the permission of the government for a legal municipal council, that is, a commune. This produced the worst of both worlds: many voters thought the elections were legal but the elected body saw itself as a revolutionary government for the whole of France. Thiers was determined to crush this with maximum force. Clemenceau and his associates still hoped to mediate between the Commune of Paris and the government, with the aim of safeguarding the principle of a republic. This attempt failed and he was lucky to escape with his life. Looking back at the end of his life on this time he remarked: *It was a good initiation into the stupidity of politics. I found myself between two sets of people both wanting my death and even that didn't cure me.*[5]

His role during the Commune had a decisive influence on Clemenceau's subsequent career for at least 20 years. On the one hand the extremely unfair account of his part on 18 March, which circulated widely among conservatives and also among middle-of-the-road republican opinion, and the fact that he had remained in Paris and sought to mediate between the Commune and the government, gave the impression that he had been a supporter of the Commune. This was one reason for the sort of tacit veto that excluded him from office. On the other hand the extreme Left never forgave him for not supporting the Commune. This became the touchstone by which a true Leftist was judged, and on this rock foundered Clemenceau's attempts in the 1880s to build up a strong radical republican party, supported by the working-class voters of Paris.

The National Assembly, with its majority of monarchists, failed to effect a restoration of the monarchy as a result of their division into supporters of different versions of monarchy, the Legitimists and Orleanists. A set of constitutional laws was drawn up in 1875, and by 1879 when MacMahon (a monarchist) resigned as President, the Republic was finally secure. But it was a very conservative version of a Republic, far removed from the First and Second Republics of 1792 and 1848, and even further from the dreams of the Commune of

1871. It was based on a compromise between the Orleanist supporters of a constitutional monarchy and the moderate republicans, who now became labelled Opportunists. Gambetta's move away from the extremism of his role in 1870–1 was crucial in this compromise. It allowed for the emergence on the extreme Left of a faction known as Radical or Radical Socialist. Clemenceau, re-elected to Parliament in 1876, for a Paris constituency that included Montmartre, soon began to bid for leadership of this faction. Gambetta was seen as the obvious leader of the republican majority, but his one attempt to form a government in 1881–2 was a fiasco. His accidental death soon afterwards gave Jules Ferry the leadership of the republicans. He was prime minister from February 1883 until brought down by Clemenceau's attack in April 1885. Ferry's main achievements were to establish a national education system free from the influence of the Catholic Church, and to push forward the policies that gave France an immense colonial empire. In both these areas he faced bitter opposition from the Right. The extreme Left criticised his educational policy as not being anticlerical enough and also opposed colonial expansion. Clemenceau's arguments against it were couched in broad terms of universal human rights that appear extremely modern, making him ahead of his time. However, it must be suspected that his real motives were different. He thought that colonial expansion would be a distraction from the goal of withstanding German pressure in Europe, and that it made Ferry accept a subordinate role in Bismarck's diplomatic network. Above all, it was an issue on which the extreme Left could combine with the Right, as happened on 30 March 1885, in one of the most dramatic parliamentary scenes in the history of the Third Republic. Challenged about a supposed French defeat in Indo-China, and attacked by Clemenceau in ferocious terms, Ferry fell from power, never to return to office. This did not stop the conquest of Indo-China continuing, however.

The division of the Radicals from more conservative republicans, and a changed electoral system, led to a revival of the monarchist Right. From having only 17 per cent of the seats in the Chamber of Deputies in 1881 they increased their share to over 36 per cent. Worse was to come with the Boulangist crisis, which posed a serious threat to the continuation of a parliamentary republic. Clemenceau was implicated here again, as General Boulanger had entered politics, being appointed minister of defence, under his patronage. Part of the Radical programme was revision of the constitution to make it more democratic: neither a Senate nor a President was part of the French tradition of republican constitutional arrangements. Boulanger, having been sacked as a minister following posturing that seemed in danger of bringing on a war with Germany for which France was completely unprepared, began a campaign for constitutional revision which had overtones of the plebiscitary system of the two Napoleonic empires. As with the two Napoleons, Boulangism allowed extreme Left and Monarchist Right to combine their forces against the middle of the road Parliamentary republic. For a brief moment in 1887–8, Boulanger, financed by elements of the Right but also appealing to left-wing voters, seemed to hold the fate of France in his hands. At this point Clemenceau drew back, cutting his links with the General, and joining the main body of the republicans, in their successful counter-attack. Boulanger himself was scared into exile, where he soon committed suicide, while the electoral system, which had contributed to his remarkable success, was changed back to that operative in 1881 with a double ballot in single member constituencies.

With hindsight this moment can be seen to mark a decisive change in Clemenceau's political stance. He accepted the constitutional arrangements of 1875 instead of attacking them as being more suited to a constitutional monarchy than to a Republic. In other ways as well he soon ceased to be the maverick challenger from the extreme Left that he had been in the 1880s. In fact his political career, like that of many of his contemporaries on the Radical side, seemed to have ended. In 1893 he lost his seat in Parliament, after a vicious campaign in which he was accused of complicity in the Panama company scandal, and of being in the pay of the British secret service. The two charges were linked by his opponents, completely without foundation. A famous cartoon showed him juggling bags of English gold, dancing as a stage entertainer, while a stereotyped Jewish face representing the businessman Cornelius Herz controlled his steps from the prompter's box. The element of truth in this was that Clemenceau had been a close associate, even a friend, of Herz who played a leading and iniquitous role in the Panama scandal. Ferdinand de Lesseps, the French engineer of the Suez Canal, tried to repeat this feat with the much more difficult scheme of a canal through the Panama isthmus. Having raised huge sums from French investors, the Panama Company was by 1886 in danger of bankruptcy. It sought special privileges from the state to help it raise more money, and bribed members of Parliament on a huge scale to ensure the passage of the legislation. When bankruptcy came anyway this corruption was revealed and played a large part in discrediting most of the republicans of Clemenceau's generation. He was not himself one who had taken bribes, but his friendship with Herz, an unsavoury adventurer born in Germany and brought up in the United States who arrived in France around 1880, placed Clemenceau

POLITICAL SYSTEM OF THE THIRD REPUBLIC

Head of State

President of the Republic: elected for a seven-year term by the two houses of Parliament (known as the National Assembly when in joint session).

Executive

Prime Minister and Cabinet: chosen by the President, but had to have the confidence of a majority of the Chamber of Deputies.

Legislature

The Senate elected for nine-year terms by electoral colleges consisting of the deputies and members of local government councils in each department.

Political parties

Political party is a term with two meanings. There is the modern sense of an organised institution with formal membership and official hierarchy: a political party, in this sense, in a democratic state, is an institution that links the political leaders in a representative assembly with the local party members, the 'militants', in the constituencies. On the other hand there is the older and vaguer sense in which one talks, say, of the Whig and Tory parties in 17th- and 18th-century England. The transition from the first to the second of these senses took place in the mid-19th century in Britain. In France it was long delayed; formed groups existed in the Chamber and the Senate, but before 1900 there were no party organisations in the country. Even after 1900 parties were weak, and had little control over the senators and deputies who belonged to them; nor did they cover the entire political spectrum. Clemenceau's position illustrates the weakness of the party organisations. He was the most prominent Radical politician in France, but he was never a leader of the Radical Party, and after 1909 not even a member of it.

at the heart of the scandal. In 1892 Baron Reinach, another financier being blackmailed by Herz, committed suicide after a mysterious interview with Clemenceau, and Herz escaped to England. The role of these almost stereotypically cosmopolitan Jewish financiers in the Panama scandal gave a great impulse to the rise of anti-Semitism in France. His close association with them, and the way that Herz, whose best

Main political parties with date of foundation

1. The Left

(a) Section Française de l'Internationale Ouvrière (SFIO) (1905): the Socialist party.

(b) Parti Républicain Socialiste (1901): the very weak organisation for those Socialists not in the SFIO, known usually as the Independent or Republican Socialists.

(c) Parti Républicain Radical et Radical-Socialistes (1901): the organised expression of the Radical tendency that had existed from the beginning of the Third Republic, and indeed, earlier.

(d) Alliance Démocratique (1901): the close relations of next below, but counted as a party of the left because of their participation in the Dreyfusard campaign.

2. The Right

(a) Fédération Républicaine (1903): descended from the conservative republicans, but separated from their former colleagues by their rejection of the Dreyfusard cause and the anti-clerical campaign that followed.

(b) Action Libérale Populaire (1902): an unsuccessful attempt to organise the Right as a Catholic party. An unkind joke said that it was so-called because it was neither active nor liberal nor popular.

(c) The Nationalist leagues, Ligue de la Patrie Française (1899): Ligue des Patriotes (1882): they were only significant in parliamentary politics from 1899–1906, although an offshoot the Ligue de l'Action Française remained in existence and was important outside Parliament.

The Right was always much less organised than the Left, and an important part of its representatives, avowedly or tacitly Royalist, remained unorganised even in the weak form of the political parties of this period.

language was American English, could be presented as the agent of the mysterious cavalry of St George, finished Clemenceau's first political career.[6]

He reinvented himself as a journalist and man of letters, producing a novel and a play, as well as a vast output of journalism. Although he had previously owned and edited a newspaper, *La Justice*, he had only rarely written in it. From

1893 to 1917 he produced an article for journalistic publication almost every day, except when holding governmental office. After 1920, although not engaged in journalism, he wrote extensively, producing four books, one of them 972 pages long. His journalism achieved real heights of eloquence in the enormous series of articles he published, mainly in the Radical newspaper *La Dépêche*, between 1899 and 1903, campaigning for the rehabilitation of Dreyfus. Alfred Dreyfus was a Jewish army officer, who had been unjustly imprisoned as a German spy in 1894. The campaign to overthrow his conviction became a political issue, which divided France more bitterly than any other during the Third Republic. Clemenceau, although not the first to take up Dreyfus' cause, was an early convert: along with that of his old friend Emile Zola it was his support that brought the case into the centre of the political stage. A crucial moment was 22 January 1898 when he found the arresting title of *J'Accuse* for Zola's open letter to the President of the Republic attacking the army officers who had fabricated evidence against Dreyfus.

Although this could not have been foreseen when he took up Dreyfus' cause, this campaign brought Clemenceau back into the centre of political life. The more conservative section of the republicans joined with the Right and political Catholicism in their support of the military authorities in the face of a mounting tide of evidence that Dreyfus was innocent, and that his conviction had been obtained and upheld by forged evidence. They argued that national security demanded defence of the military establishment against the rights of an individual. While extremists on the Left adopted an anti-militarist position, Clemenceau and the main body of Dreyfus defenders insisted that justice for Dreyfus did not mean an attack on the army. As he said in a speech at Zola's trial:

There was nothing more absurd than the accusation that we are insulting the army. We honour the army by requiring it to respect the law … If, absorbed by the idea of national defence civil society abandoned itself to military servitude, than we might still have some soil to defend, but we would have abandoned everything which had given France her glory and renown in the world, ideas of liberty and justice.[7]

The outcome of the long and bitter conflict was a presidential pardon for Dreyfus, and the political victory of the left-wing coalition that had fought his case. This coalition went from the revolutionary Socialists on the Left, through the Radical Socialists (Clemenceau's tendency) and Radicals to those moderate (conservative) republicans who had fought for Dreyfus' cause. This line of division came to remain basic to French politics for the rest of Clemenceau's career and longer. This coalition was known as the *Bloc des Gauches*, a term coined by Clemenceau in 1891 when he declared that the French Revolution was a *bloc;* that is it must be taken as a whole, incorporating all its aspects, including the massacres and the Terror.[9]

Whether we like it or not, whether it pleases us or shocks us, the French Revolution is a bloc from which nothing can be separated, because historical truth does not permit it.
CLEMENCEAU[8]

Clemenceau himself had still not returned to Parliament when the victory of the *Bloc des Gauches* was confirmed in the 1902 elections, but soon afterwards he was elected to the Senate for the department of the Var in the south. From then onwards he again played a leading role in politics, especially in the campaign for the separation of Church and State, depriving the Catholic Church of the support it had received from the State since Napoleon's Concordat of 1801.

In 1906 he came to ministerial office for the first time at the age of 64; at first he was minister of the interior in a government headed by Sarrien, but from October 1906 to July 1909 he was prime minister, at the head of one of the longest-lived of any Third Republic government. Up to that moment Clemenceau had always been far to the Left of the political spectrum. But he had been neither a revolutionary nor a collectivist Socialist. His arrival in office shortly followed the emergence on his left of a unified Socialist party, calling itself the SFIO, the French section of the Socialist International. Adopting, at least in theory, a dogmatic Marxist approach this new organisation forbade its members to take part in 'bourgeois' governments, a doctrine to which it adhered with the exception of the period of the war until 1936. This meant that Clemenceau's Radicals were no longer on the extreme Left of the political spectrum, but on the centre Left. Several bitter struggles with a trade union movement that compensated for its numerical weakness with rhetorical extremism and violence brought him the reputation of a strong man who would use all the force of the state to defend law and order. As he said himself, his position made him *le premier flic de France*, 'the top cop'. But in French terms it did not make him a reactionary or a Rightist. The Right was defined by its defence of the Catholic Church and its distaste for the Republic. Clemenceau, an atheist and anticlerical, firmly defended the separation of Church and State. Although he had in his early years criticised the details of the constitution, he now defended it against critics. To those who argued that it meant weak and ephemeral governments, he pointed to the stability of his own period in office.

Although not in power between 1909 and his return in the darkest days of the war in November 1917, he played an important part in French politics throughout. In January 1912 he overthrew Joseph Caillaux, the prime minister who had concluded an agreement with Germany in which France paid for the right to make Morocco a protectorate by conceding territory in Central Africa to Germany, but he tried and failed to prevent the election of Raymond Poincaré as President. To promote his own political views, in 1913 he founded a newspaper, *L'Homme Libre*, which he edited and contributed to almost every day. After the outbreak of war the influence of his articles there was considerable. His political position was strengthened when he was elected president of two important Senate committees, for War and for Foreign Affairs. Under the political system of the Third Republic, these committees had a very important position, never more so than during the war. He made very few public speeches before November 1917, but through the Senate committees and his newspaper, he established a position on the political stage that meant that he could not be ignored. Although invited to join the government on several occasions, he refused unless he could have full power as prime minister.

JOSEPH CAILLAUX (1863–1944)
As Minister of Finance Caillaux had played an important role in Clemenceau's first ministry. but his attempt as prime minister in 1911 to restore good relations with Germany after the Agadir crisis led Clemenceau to bring down his government. Henceforth he stood for a policy of reconciliation with Germany which opened him to charges of treasonable activity. Arrested in January 1918 as part of the campaign against defeatism, he was only tried in 1920. Sentenced to three years' imprisonment and loss of political rights, he was only able to resume his political career when amnestied by the new left-wing government in 1925. It has been said that in November 1917 the choice was between a Caillaux government to seek peace and a Clemenceau government to fight the war to the end. It is a sign of the complexity of French politics that these two opposing symbols were both Radicals, although Clemenceau was no longer a party member.

By the summer of 1917 the war was going very badly for the Allies. The domestic political situation in France was also extremely worrying. Although the Sacred Union, proclaimed in 1914 as the union of all political parties in support of the war, remained formally in place, it was clearly being challenged behind the scenes. There was a wave of strikes in the early months of 1917, and the minority within the SFIO which wished to withdraw support for the government was gaining ground: in the event the minority only became the majority in October 1918, but socialist participation in the government was clearly under threat. Even more serious was the failure of the Nivelle offensive in April 1917. General Robert Nivelle, who had replaced Joffre as commander-in-chief of the French armies on the Western Front, had promised the government that he would achieve the decisive breakthrough which had been sought throughout two years of trench warfare. Instead, the enormous sacrifices he demanded from his troops achieved the smallest of advances. He had demonstrated all over again that the defence had the advantage in the conditions and with the military equipment of the Western Front in 1917. But the failure of the Nivelle offensive came as the last straw to the troops involved, producing serious mutinies in May and June. Nivelle himself was removed from command on 15 May, being replaced by General Philippe Pétain whose defensive tactics had saved Verdun in 1916. He was already convinced of the futility of frontal infantry attacks, and dealt with the mutinies by a judicious combination of conciliation and fairness. The troops on the front line never mutinied, and the Germans were unaware of the gravity of the situation. But for several weeks the French army in the sector involved was not an effective fighting force, and it did not engage in a major offensive on the Western Front for almost 12 months. As spring turned to summer in 1917 the Allies found themselves in a desperately worrying situation. It was true that the United States had entered the war on their side, and in the long run this greatly strengthened them, but since the revolution in March, Russia was rapidly ceasing to be an effective combatant. Clemenceau, like many others, had welcomed the fall of the Tsar and had hoped that the liberals would galvanise the Russian army. Even two months later, with the Socialist Kerensky replacing Miliukov as the dominant figure, such hopes could be seen to be hollow. The term 'defeatism' passed from the Russian language into French to denote the enemy within, who was sapping the will to continue the war: similar forces were, it was argued, at work in France. American entry into the war made it all the more important for Germany to use its temporary advantage to achieve victory before American potential could be brought to bear. Germany hoped to do this through the U-boat campaign to cut off food and raw materials from across the Atlantic, while the Russian collapse allowed its military strength to be transferred from the Eastern to the Western Front. Another German ploy was to take advantage of the liberal systems of government in the Allied countries by financing opposition groups to demand peace. Peace terms could be presented as deceptively moderate in a general way, until, when the details were finally exposed, they revealed a peace which would give Germany complete domination of the European continent. This process worked perfectly in Russia, although it took about 11 months from the despatch of Lenin and his Bolshevik colleagues from Switzerland to Petrograd for the signing of the Treaty of Brest-Litovsk in March 1918. The same methods were adopted against Britain (in Ireland) and France but with very little success. German attempts to influence French opinion by buying French newspapers achieved nothing except the deaths of some unfortunates convicted of unlawful contact with the enemy. Only the little men (and women – Mata Hari) suffered such fates. Two important politicians, Jean Malvy and Caillaux had their reputations tarnished and suffered trial and imprisonment for contact with the enemy, or, in Malvy's case, negligence in preventing such contacts. Aristide Briand, an even more important figure, was too cautious to expose himself to similar charges, but he also was tempted in autumn 1917 into contact with a German emissary making misleading offers of peace talks.

Whatever their imprudence, neither Malvy, Briand nor Caillaux were in any sense German agents, but it was his attacks on them in the summer of 1917 that at last brought Clemenceau to power. On 22 July he launched a devastating attack on Malvy in the Senate, publishing his speech in a pamphlet entitled *l'Antipatriotisme devant le Sénat*. From this time onwards he had the support of the journalists of the extreme Right, Barrès, Daudet and Maurras, who did talk of treason as the reason for the failure of the Nivelle offensive of April. Although Malvy survived for a few weeks, he resigned at the end of August, bringing down the Ribot government. Ribot was followed as prime minister by his own minister of war, Painlevé, formerly a professor of mathematics. His weak and short-lived government coincided with the disastrous period of Italy's defeat at Caporetto and the Bolshevik revolution in Russia. In France there were more accusations of treason in high places: the implications were that Caillaux, Malvy and possibly Briand were involved. The major question in 1917 was whether France should continue the war or make peace on the best terms it could. Clemenceau forced into the open the fact of Briand's discreet German contacts in an article in *L'Homme Enchainé*.

Clemenceau has been attacked for his supposed role in preventing a peace of compromise in 1917. But no such peace was possible on terms acceptable to the great majority in France. Painlevé's faltering from one crisis to the next convinced many that Clemenceau would soon be asked to head the government. In October Poincaré said he thought that: 'Clemenceau is indicated by public opinion because he wished to see things through to the end with regard to the war and the judicial affairs and that, in these circumstances, I did not have the right to exclude him simply because of his attitude towards me.' Poincaré called Clemenceau in on the following day, noting 'The Tiger arrives. He is fatter and his deafness has increased. His intelligence is intact. But what about his health, and his willpower? I fear that one or the other may have changed for the worse, and I feel more and more the risk of this adventure, but this *diable d'homme* has all patriots on his side, and if I do not call on him his legendary strength would make any alternative cabinet weak.' They had a friendly conversation and Poincaré was reassured. Clemenceau told him that he believed that Pétain was the best military leader and he was retained

RAYMOND POINCARÉ (1860–1934)
Poincaré's political position was close to Clemenceau's, especially with regard to Germany. But their personal antipathy was extreme, and their careers evolved in counterpoint. Poincaré rose to prominence after 1893 when Clemenceau was ousted, while the Dreyfus Affair eclipsed him as it restored Clemenceau to power. President of the Republic from 1913 to 1920, Poincaré sought to strengthen the role of the president, with some success until he appointed Clemenceau prime minister: thereafter he lost all influence until he returned to Parliament after Clemenceau's resignation. He was the dominant figure for most of the 1920s, being prime minister 1922–4 and 1926–9. Throughout this period he criticised the weakness of the peace settlement, while Clemenceau responded by arguing that the weakness resulted from Poincaré's failure to insist on German compliance with its terms.

as commander of the French army on the Western Front until the end of the war.[10]

Clemenceau himself took the Ministry of War, and brought back Pichon to the foreign ministry. The cabinet was dominated by undistinguished Radical and Centre-Left politicians. Apart from Clemenceau himself, and Etienne Clémentel, who added a host of other economic responsibilities to his main charge as Minister of Commerce, the most important figure was the businessman Louis Loucheur, at the Ministry of Munitions; Loucheur was not a party politician, nor even a member of parliament. The press was generally favourable as was the Right, although none of its members was in the cabinet. On 20 November the new cabinet met the Chamber of Deputies and Clemenceau gave his brief but eloquent ministerial declaration that the whole of France, workers in the factories or tilling the fields, old and young, were fighting against modern forms of ancient barbarism. *We will avoid weakness, as we will avoid violence. All the guilty before courts-martial. The soldier in the courtroom, united with the soldier in battle. No more pacifist campaigns, no more German intrigues. Neither treason, nor semi-treason: the war. Nothing but the war. Our armies will not be caught between fire from two sides. Justice will be done. The country will know that it is defended.*[11]

He achieved extraordinary rhetorical effect in these staccato phrases, the style exactly expressing the thought, as his programme avoided anything beyond the need to continue the terrible struggle. The atmosphere was now quite different from that of 1917; even when the Germans almost broke through the Western Front in the spring of 1918, French morale did not waver. France was determined to fight on under Clemenceau's leadership.

3

The End of the War

On 16 November 1917, almost exactly one year before the armistice that ended the war with Germany, Clemenceau formed his second ministry. He was now 76, but this was the year that placed him in the pantheon of French national heroes. His incarnation of the French will to survive through the last dreadful months was expressed in his new nickname, Père-la-Victoire (Old Man Victory). Impossible to translate, it encompasses the feelings of affection, confidence and respect which he now inspired. Père so-and-so is the nickname often given to an old man who is regarded by his fellow villagers with friendly respect, often a prosperous peasant or craftsman. In Clemenceau's case it indicates how he had completely outstepped limits of social class, sectarian politics or educational and cultural distinctions. It suggests his common touch. His speeches might make classical allusions, as in his inaugural speech when he said he might have to account for his mistakes, at the tribunal of Aeacus, Rhadamanthos and Minos, but he managed also to talk in a way everyone could understand, direct and earthy. Above all, his frequent visits to the front line gained him general respect. The infantry soldiers of the trenches, (or *poilus*) gave him the new nickname which illustrated a different side to his character than that which earned him the sobriquet 'the Tiger'.

Some historical accounts have persisted in expressing the bitterness of Clemenceau's contemporary opponents and have presented him as a dictator forcing by means of harsh repression a reluctant populace to fight on against its will. But this view is not tenable. Pierre Renouvin has pointed out that Clemenceau's success in making the French parliamentary system provide an effective and strong war government was only possible because of the support of public opinion. He concluded: 'previous cabinets had appeared more conscientious than energetic, and the public welcomed a programme showing a determination to rule … A wave of confidence, springing from the very soul of the country, cleared the way for the government, and swept aside the whims of the parliamentary opposition and the hesitations of critical minds.'[1] Clemenceau's domination of the cabinet was remarked on by the British ambassador: 'Clemenceau is the only man in the government: whether it be Pichon, Leygues, or anybody else who speaks to you, it is Clemenceau alone who can give a definite answer on any subject.'[2]

At no time did the government come anywhere near defeat in the Chamber. During the war the weakest position was the vote of 18 January 1918 of 368 to 155. After the two most dramatic debates, that of 8 March in which the Socialists launched a bitter attack on Clemenceau for his 'provocation of the working class', and that of 4 June after the great German advance in Champagne, the voting was 368 to 115 and 377 to 110 respectively. After the war the government majorities were somewhat reduced, but there was never any danger of the Chamber overthrowing the cabinet.

The fact that the Sacred Union was formally abandoned and the Clemenceau government condemned by the Socialist party, was an element of parliamentary strength, not weakness. Whereas earlier governments had sought to conciliate the Socialists there was now no need for such tenderness. There was a clear-cut confrontation between supporters and opponents and the opposition was shown to be only a small part of the Chamber, made up of the Socialists, some Republican-Socialists and a number of left-wing Radicals.

'But for the war Clemenceau would have finished as a grumpy old man haunting the corridors of the Senate and writing bad journalism. The war shaped him into the Archetypical Frenchman, able to seize victory in his grasp, and then in part, to let its fruits escape him, in the way that Rodin sculpts a magnificent statue out of the unformed rock.'
ALBERT THIBAUDET[3]

Clemenceau's political position became more secure as the possibility of German victory receded. But for the first six months of 1918 a German breakthrough on the Western Front seemed more likely than at any time since autumn 1914. There had been no serious fighting on the Eastern Front since the end of 1916, and the Treaty of Brest-Litovsk was signed on 3 March 1918. Food and raw materials from the Ukraine and Russia offered Germany some possibility of escape from the stranglehold of the Allied economic blockade. Although America's entry into the war brought economic and financial support to the Allies, direct military help from the American army played a very limited part until late summer of 1918. This was the result of the American refusal, except in the case of the most dire emergency, to allow their troops to reinforce the British or the French armies. They insisted on the American army fighting as a separate army, something that remained impossible until just before the end. It was the weary veterans, reinforced by conscripted boys, 18–19 years old, of the British and French armies who resisted the last of Ludendorff's onslaughts, and began at last to push back the German army from the line it had established across northern France in 1914. But before the turning-point in August 1918, Ludendorff came very near to winning his last gambler's throw, and defeating the Allies before American strength could be brought into play. This was when the German attack, launched near Amiens on 21 March, at the point where the northern British-held section of the front joined that held by the French, looked as though it would lead to the separation of British and French forces, with the British retreating back to the Channel ports, while the French retreated south to protect Paris. There is no room here for discussion of the military operations, but Clemenceau's vital role in preventing this disaster must be mentioned. This took place at a meeting at the little town of Doullens, near Amiens, on 26 March, where Clemenceau and Poincaré met Lord Milner, representing the British government, and the two army commanders, Haig and Pétain. Pétain was very pessimistic, stating that the Germans were about to totally defeat the British, and then they would be able to defeat the French.

HENRI-PHILIPPE PÉTAIN (1856–1951)
Only a colonel in 1914, almost at the end of an undistinguished career, Pétain became a national hero as the saviour of Verdun in 1916. His rejection of offensive strategy and his natural caution made him commander-in-chief after the failure of the Nivelle offensive, a post he retained until the end of the war. Foch's attempts to play a political role in 1919 led to his eclipse; Pétain, now a Marshal, became the dominant military figure in the inter-war period. After the defeat of 1940 he was given total political power as head of State in the collaborationist Vichy government.

As Clemenceau said to his aide Mordacq: *After an interview like that, you need an iron-band spirit to retain your confidence.* His own reaction was to seek to inspire confidence by visiting Parliament to walk up and down the antechambers *with a smile on my face*.[4]

The German offensive had revealed the inadequacy of arrangements for Allied co-operation, as up to this moment there had been no overall commander-in-chief. The Doullens meeting gave Foch the position of Allied commander-in-chief on the Western Front, a subordination which the British had previously rejected: that it was now accepted was, as well as the extreme crisis, because of Clemenceau's tact, and his personal relationship with Milner. In the event, the Allied front was re-established and the offensive was contained as had every other achieved by either side on the Western Front since 1914. Still other German attacks were launched in April and May; the British and French were struggling desperately to find enough men to replace their casualties. The German military machine seemed to be more powerful then ever. Clutching at straws, the Allies got involved at this time in elaborate schemes to overthrow the Bolsheviks so as to revive the Eastern Front. Recognising the improbability of this, some in the British government contemplated a future in which Germany had won the war on land and controlled the whole of Europe. Lord Milner wrote to Lloyd George on 9 June: 'We must be prepared for France and Italy both being beaten to their knees. In that case the Germano-Austro-Turko-Bulgar block will be master of all Europe and northern and central Asia up to the point at which Japan steps in to bar the way.'[5]

Even rejecting such pessimism there was still no sign of the impending German collapse and Allied planning concentrated on preparing for the campaign of 1919. But in reality the German attack of 15 July was Ludendorff's last throw. It was defeated, and the Allies began very slowly to make gains. The 'black day' of the German army was 8 August. Ludendorff lost his nerve and began the reassessment which was to bring the German High Command to tell the political authorities that they must request an armistice. Over the months before that time Clemenceau had increased his visits to the fighting troops, getting as close to the front line as possible, frequently exposing himself to danger. In this way he was far removed from the journalists such as Barrès and Gustave Hervé, who penned ferocious diatribes against the Hun from the safety of their Parisian desks. Clemenceau's wartime speeches had immense emotional impact because of this first hand exposure to the front. He himself at a speech inaugurating the war memorial in his native village, Ste Hermine, in October 1921, described a visit to the front before one of the last German attacks: *Hidden in the folds of the ground, hairy heads, powdered with the dusty soil of Champagne, emerged fantastically from invisible machine-gun emplacements ... They greeted us! Sometimes only with their eyes, which burned with an invincible resolution. Impenetrable blocks of heroism, they were a rear guard, whose orders were to get themselves killed to the last man without ceasing fire ... Those lower down had time to prepare ... They came to meet the visitor, vague shapes all white with the dust, who made the gesture of lining up to give the military salute while their leader stepped forward and in staccato tones shouted out. 'First company, second batallion, third regiment, present'! And with his rough hand he offered a little bouquet of chalky flowers ... Ah, those frail dried-up stalks. The Vendée will see them; for I have promised that they will go to the grave with me ... And the old man, choking with a superhuman emotion, grasped with all his strength that iron hand, and could only stammer incoherent words and swear that that little bunch of flowers, without colour and without sap, a pledge of the most sublime self-sacrifice to an ideal, would never leave him. He who has not lived through such moments does not know what life can give.* The bouquet was preserved in his study until he died, and then was placed in his coffin.[6]

ooooo

The task of preparing armistice terms in the late summer of 1918 was one for which the Allies were unprepared, due to the sudden collapse of the Central Powers. Even as late as August of that year the Allies had been anticipating that the campaign would continue into 1919. However, one after the other, they sought peace. The Bulgarians were first to request an armistice, and were out of the war by 29 September. On 5 October German and Austrian notes to President Wilson followed, requesting an armistice founded on the Fourteen Points. Turkey was out of the war by 31 October, followed by Austria-Hungary on 3 November and Germany on 11 November. In Germany's case negotiations were top level and more complex. Germany still had some fighting capacity, and the Allies were not sure how far it could be pushed. At the same time they were resolved that any terms agreed would not allow the German army's withdrawal to a better tactical position that might enable it to resume fighting. So the Allies' minimum terms were to prevent Germany resuming the war as well as to provide the chief desiderata for the eventual peace settlement.

The negotiation of the peace terms by the Allies

PRESIDENT WILSON'S FOURTEEN POINTS, 8 JANUARY 1918

The program of the world's peace, therefore, is our program; and that program, the only possible program, as we see it, is this:

I. Open covenants of peace, openly arrived at, after which there shall be no private international understandings of any kind but diplomacy shall proceed always frankly and in the public view.

II. Absolute freedom of navigation upon the seas, outside territorial waters, alike in peace and in war, except as the seas may be closed in whole or in part by international action for the enforcement of international covenants.

III. The removal, so far as possible, of all economic barriers and the establishment of an equality of trade conditions among all the nations consenting to the peace and associating themselves for its maintenance.

IV. Adequate guarantees given and taken that national armaments will be reduced to the lowest point consistent with domestic safety.

V. A free, open-minded, and absolutely impartial adjustment of all colonial claims, based upon a strict observance of the principle that in determining all such questions of sovereignty the interests of the populations concerned must have equal weight with the equitable claims of the government whose title is to be determined.

VI. The evacuation of all Russian territory and such a settlement of all questions affecting Russia as will secure the best and freest cooperation of the other nations of the world in obtaining for her an unhampered and unembarrassed opportunity for the independent determination of her own political development and national policy and assure her of a sincere welcome into the society of free nations under institutions of her own choosing; and, more than a welcome, assistance also of every kind that she may need and may herself desire. The treatment accorded Russia by her sister nations in the months to come will be the acid test of their good will, of their comprehension of her needs as distinguished from their own interests, and of their intelligent and unselfish sympathy.

VII. Belgium, the whole world will agree, must be evacuated and restored, without any attempt to limit the sovereignty which she enjoys in common with all other free nations. No other single act will serve as this will serve to restore confidence among the nations in the laws which they

have themselves set and determined for the government of their relations with one another. Without this healing act the whole structure and validity of international law is forever impaired.

VIII. All French territory should be freed and the invaded portions restored, and the wrong done to France by Prussia in 1871 in the matter of Alsace-Lorraine, which has unsettled the peace of the world for nearly fifty years, should be righted, in order that peace may once more be made secure in the interest of all.

IX. A readjustment of the frontiers of Italy should be effected along clearly recognizable lines of nationality.

X. The peoples of Austria-Hungary, whose place among the nations we wish to see safeguarded and assured, should be accorded the freest opportunity to autonomous development.

XI. Rumania, Serbia, and Montenegro should be evacuated; occupied territories restored; Serbia accorded free and secure access to the sea; and the relations of the several Balkan states to one another determined by friendly counsel along historically established lines of allegiance and nationality; and international guarantees of the political and economic independence and territorial integrity of the several Balkan states should be entered into.

XII. The Turkish portion of the present Ottoman Empire should be assured a secure sovereignty, but the other nationalities which are now under Turkish rule should be assured an undoubted security of life and an absolutely unmolested opportunity of autonomous development, and the Dardanelles should be permanently opened as a free passage to the ships and commerce of all nations under international guarantees.

XIII. An independent Polish state should be erected which should include the territories inhabited by indisputably Polish populations, which should be assured a free and secure access to the sea, and whose political and economic independence and territorial integrity should be guaranteed by international covenant.

XIV. A general association of nations must be formed under specific covenants for the purpose of affording mutual guarantees of political independence and territorial integrity to great and small states alike.

foreshadowed their later disputes about the terms to be imposed on Germany during the peace negotiations themselves. President Wilson had been approached by the Germans on his own, not the Allies as a whole. This was made possible by the United States' role as an 'associated co-belligerent', not formally allied to the others. President Wilson was able, therefore, to threaten that he would dictate his own terms in a separate peace agreement. However, after paying lip-service to Wilson's vague shibboleths the Allies succeeded in reasserting their influence.

On 5 October, when news of the German note arrived, the Allied premiers were meeting in the Supreme War Council in Paris. They made the decision to ask their military advisers to draw up proposals whereby the evacuation of all occupied territory by the Germans, along with the cessation of submarine warfare would be secured. This would entail Germany's withdrawal behind the Rhine, but no Allied advance into German territory, including Alsace-Lorraine. Advice was requested from the permanent military representatives on the Supreme War Council, a group meeting at Versailles. They were second-string figures, bypassed after Foch's appointment as supreme Allied commander. Foch intervened by writing to Clemenceau on 8 October, giving his own views on the terms. The British reaction to Foch's terms was that they were in effect unconditional surrender. Lloyd George reported of the meeting that Foch's terms amounted to saying 'No' with a swagger. Foch's terms differed from those of the Versailles Committee in his demand for Allied occupation of the left bank of the Rhine and three bridgeheads on the other side. At the Supreme War Council meeting on 8 October Clemenceau supported Foch but was determined to assert control over final policy decisions against Foch and Poincaré. For at this point Poincaré also intervened, expressing his opposition to an armistice that would, he wrote, hamstring the victorious advance of the Allied armies to Berlin. Clemenceau was infuriated as he was determined to end the war at the first moment it could be ended in victory. As he later said to his secretary Martet: *At the first request for an armistice, I nearly went mad, mad with joy. It was finished. I had seen too much of the front, too many of those water-filled holes where men had lived for four years ... M Poincaré could keep calm, and write me his little letters – 'you should not hamstring etc' – all in his tiny cramped handwriting ...*[7]

An angry exchange of letters ensued, and Clemenceau threatened to resign. Poincaré eventually withdrew and accepted his exclusion from the decision making process, relinquishing further attempts at direct influence over Clemenceau, but through maintaining contact with Foch encouraging his opposition to Clemenceau. A week later Foch began his many attempts to take on a political role by requesting

MARSHAL FERDINAND FOCH (1851–1929)

Foch's Catholic background held back his career before 1914, although Clemenceau had appointed him director of the École de Guerre during his first ministry. Removal of incompetent generals brought him near to the top of the military hierarchy by the end of 1914. But Joffre's fall sidelined him temporarily, while Pétain's defence of Verdun made him the national hero. However, the crisis of March 1918 allowed Clemenceau to appoint Foch as Allied commander-in-chief on the Western Front, with Haig, Pétain and Pershing as respective chiefs of the British, French and American armies. In reality, Foch could only persuade and co-ordinate: he certainly did not have the power, for instance, to remove Pershing as Clemenceau wanted him to do. Nevertheless, Foch's strategic vision certainly played a part in victory, although the bulk of the fighting that broke the German army was done by the British. Victory brought Foch immense prestige, which made it impossible for Clemenceau to simply ignore his repeated attempts to influence political decisions. After 1919 he played only a ceremonial role, while Pétain continued to direct French military thinking.

a Foreign Office official's help in preparing the terms of the armistice. He argued that it was essential for him to know the government's peace proposals, and in particular their views on the status of the Rhineland, whether it was to be annexed, or become an autonomous neutral area. He only envisaged these two alternatives. Clemenceau's answer was firm, but less insulting than that he had made to Poincaré. He stated that only the government was authorised by the constitution to deal with Foch's questions: political decisions had to be distinct from advice on military matters. Another opponent of the armistice was Pétain. Clemenceau and Foch, however, were the only ones on the French side who were involved in the armistice negotiations. Clemenceau insisted that Foch was there to give advice on military concerns and that the politicians were there to make the decisions. It appears that the cabinet was not consulted. Clemenceau informed the president of the External Affairs Chamber that he and Pichon had been given *carte blanche* by the cabinet and that they had agreed not to be informed for the time being. So information was certainly not going to be communicated to a Parliamentary committee.

President Wilson had agreed to send Colonel Edward House, his representative, to participate in discussions with the Allied governments. Between 20 October and 5 November the detailed terms of the armistice were agreed at a series of Supreme War Council meetings. They were based on the documents presented by various military and naval commanders. The result was a formidable ultimatum aiming to ensure that Germany would be unable to enter again into the war, very different from what the Germans had hoped for after their appeal to Wilson. In the discussion of the armistice by the Allies, Clemenceau acted as a restraining influence, aiming to not upset Wilson. Until the hard bargaining of March and April 1919 Clemenceau seems to have thought that the United States was more likely than Britain to support France's demands. House, who was on very friendly terms with Clemenceau, often gave the impression that the United States was ready to accept the French case. Lloyd George was very much opposed. His most adamant opposition was to the second of the Fourteen Points, the freedom of the seas. Clemenceau supported him in this stand but the debate gives the impression that the French could not understand why so much energy was expended on the discussion of issues that seemed to be concerned with Anglo-American relations rather that the German armistice. House concentrated on gaining the acceptance by the Allies of the general aspirations of Wilson's Fourteen Points, open covenants, freedom of the seas and removal of trade barriers. In effect freedom of the seas was rejected and the other points were accepted in the belief that they did not entail precise commitments. Lloyd George said that he had no objections to any of the other clauses. They were wide enough to allow the participants to place their own interpretations upon them.

House did not support either Foch's reservations about the stiff naval terms proposed by the British admiralty or the British objections to French proposals concerning the occupation of the Rhineland. He in fact took little interest in the precise clauses that were being outlined by the British and French. He wrote to Wilson that Clemenceau gave his word of honour that France would withdraw after the peace conditions had been fulfilled. Thus the terms of the French soldiers and British sailors were incorporated into the armistice. Balfour, however, was able to delete a clause that the German army in the East should withdraw to the Polish frontier of

1772, which would have appeared to prejudge the question of the future boundaries of Poland. House did not object, either, to the interpretation of Wilson's vague reference to the restoration of Belgium and the French territory that had been invaded as a basis for reparation claims against Germany. The final peace terms were to show just how far this interpretation could be stretched.

Allied acceptance that the terms of the armistice were based on Wilson's programme was made clear when House said that the President had insisted on Germany accepting all his speeches, and from these they could establish almost any point that anyone wished against Germany. The end result was that the extreme French programme went through with very few changes. This left Germany helpless in the face of the Allies, and Lloyd George argued for less severe terms, believing that Germany would not agree. Clemenceau countered that *the situation of the Allies vis-à-vis the enemy had never been so crushing before. The American effectives were enormous. Tomorrow the Allies would be able to march across Austria against Germany. He had little doubt that the first reply of the German government would be to refuse our terms, but as we increased our advantage they would concede them.*[8]

Lloyd George recorded his disquiet and reluctantly allowed himself to be overruled. The French proved to be right sooner that they had expected because internal developments in Germany meant that any further German resistance became impossible. The liberal Prince Max of Baden was appointed Chancellor on 3 October, transforming the Empire into a constitutional monarchy. But within days the revolutionary avalanche began to sweep away the whole structure of Wilhelmine Germany. Before the armistice could be signed a naval mutiny sparked off violent revolution and the new chancellor handed over power to the socialist leader Friedrich Ebert, while another socialist proclaimed the republic. By the first week in November there was no possibility of resistance, whatever the terms.

There were good reasons for ending the war as soon as possible even at the cost of allowing the German army to march home unconquered. Apart from humanitarian considerations, continued fighting would have emphasised the weakness of the French army compared with those of Britain and the United States. In addition the prospect of the occupation and administration of large areas of Germany was daunting. This had seemed to be a possibility when governmental authority in Germany appeared to be threatened with collapse, but was abandoned with relief when it became clear that the provisional republican government had gained sufficient control to comply with the terms of the armistice. On 7 November the German authorities sent a delegation across the front line to receive the armistice terms. It was headed by the Centre Party politician Mathias Erzberger and contained only low-level army and navy officers. The High Command kept themselves far away from any responsibility, although they had over the last month insisted on the need for an armistice. In contrast the Allies sent their supreme commander Foch with his assistant Weygand. The two sides met in a railway carriage in the Forest of Compiègne, a location underlining how close to Paris the front line remained even at this stage. German protests at the terms were not totally disregarded. In response to the plea that maintenance of the blockade meant starvation for the German people, the Allies agreed that they would envisage supplying Germany with food during the armistice, although they promised nothing. Minor changes were made in the disarmament requirements, as the Germans warned of the need to safeguard against the danger of a Bolshevik revolution. After two days needed for the communication of the terms of the government in Berlin, and a final night of bargaining, the armistice was signed at 5.10 a.m. on the morning of 11 November 1918, to take effect at 11 a.m. Clemenceau could be satisfied with the strong bargaining counters he had gained, in spite of later criticism from political and military leaders. Already on 5 November, with peace in sight, Clemenceau had announced to the Chamber the armistice with Austria, and recalled that he was the last survivor of the deputies who had signed the protest against the loss of Alsace-Lorraine. Now on 11 November he read out the terms of the armistice, welcomed *Alsace-Lorraine, at last returned to France, one and indivisible, as our fathers called her.*[10] The entire chamber burst into the Marseillaise, as the ceremonial guns began to sound.

France, formerly the warrior of God now the warrior of humanity, always the warrior of the ideal, will recover her place in the world, to continue her magnificent unending race in pursuit of human progress.
CLEMENCEAU[9]

Between the armistice and the start of the Peace Conference in Paris on 12 January 1919, two months elapsed, and it was another two months before the questions vital to France were thrashed out between Clemenceau, Wilson and Lloyd George. Clemenceau wrote to Lloyd George that it would be advisable to *let the German revolution settle down a little so that we can see what we have to deal with*.[11] The arrival of President Wilson was awaited, and in addition there were many ceremonial visits and celebrations to be carried out. Lloyd George also wished to hold the British elections. In the interim the time could be spent in sounding out British and American intentions and formulating the French demands and presenting them to the Allies. Various individuals and organisations set to work on the French proposals, although Clemenceau was careful to avoid commitment to any one particular scheme. Speaking in the Chamber of Deputies on 29 December 1918 he reminded them that the peace must be a compromise between all the Allies, and refused to make a statement about French peace proposals.

André Tardieu was told to extract a precise programme from the academic body, the Comité d'Études, set up in 1916 to provide background studies for a future peace settlement, which had so far drawn few conclusions. At the Quai d'Orsay, Philippe Berthelot developed outline proposals dealing with the substantive demands of the French besides procedures and organisation of the Peace Conference. Clemenceau was reported to find Berthelot's memoranda absurd: nonetheless they were presented to Britain and the United States, in slightly different versions, at the end of 1918. They were strikingly similar to the French proposals that Clemenceau was to fight for in the March and April of 1919. Germany was to relinquish large areas which were mainly inhabited by non-Germans, but the principle of self-determination was abandoned for the Saar, and insofar as was necessary to enable Poland and Czechoslovakia to become strong states.

PHILIPPE BERTHELOT (1866–1934)
Assistant director of political and commercial affairs, Berthelot was in fact in 1918–1919 the chief permanent official of the Ministry of Foreign Affairs, his nominal superior, Pierre de Margerie, being incapacitated by illness. His close relationship with Briand made Clemenceau suspicious of him at first, but he soon came to appreciate his extraordinary abilities.

Propositions for a preliminary peace with Germany stated that there were three essential questions. First, the military neutralisation of the Rhine's left bank, along with the return to France of the territory taken in 1815 as well as in 1871, that is, the Saar and Alsace-Lorraine. The second question concerned the creation of a strong anti-German and anti-Bolshevik Poland. Thirdly it was stated that Germany's political system would be for them to decide, but also that federalist tendencies would be fostered. These proposals were notably more moderate than those put forward in November by Foch, and tallied with a plan drafted by Gabriel Hanotaux (who had no official position) and submitted by Foch in November 1918. Here the essential element was the plan for the incorporation of the Rhinelanders in the Allied armies. Foch argued that this was the only way to rectify the imbalance between Germany and the Allies. Later Foch argued for a less ambitious second version, supporting the creation of an 'autonomous' Rhineland state or states. Clemenceau's views were reported by the British ambassador on 14 December 1918 as follows: 'he said that the Rhine was a natural boundary of Gaul and Germany and that it ought to be made the German boundary now, the territory between the Rhine and the French frontier being made into an independent state whose neutrality should be guaranteed by the great powers. I can see that he intends to press very strongly. Foch had put forward a suggestion that an independent army should be raised in those parts for its defence, but Clemenceau had vetoed that on the grounds that it was unnecessary and dangerous. He tells me however Foch looks upon it as a military necessity and will press for it at the Conference.'[12]

When Clemenceau and Foch visited London at the beginning of December, he was pointedly absent from the meeting at which Foch presented his plan to the British. Lloyd George said this was because Clemenceau believed Foch would present such ideas more persuasively with his prestige as commander-in-chief. However, it is more probable that Clemenceau wished Foch to appreciate the British lack of sympathy with such ideas. It would also he believed, demonstrate Clemenceau's moderation (in contrast to Foch) to Lloyd George. In informal private conversations Clemenceau and Lloyd George also discussed the Middle Eastern settlement. Many of the formal meetings concerned plans to bring the Kaiser to trial, which were supported by Clemenceau, but more strongly by Lloyd George. Procedural matters were discussed although those proposed were different from those in fact later adopted. Paris was agreed as the venue for the Peace Conference, with Clemenceau presiding. At this stage the idea persisted that they could divide the work into a 'preliminary peace', laying down the settlement's main lines which could be quickly agreed. Then the full Conference would meet to arrange the details and draw up the final treaty. Clemenceau strongly opposed any suggestion that the Bolsheviks should be invited to the Peace Conference. That part of the settlement would have to await more clarity as the situation evolved. After these inter-Allied meetings Clemenceau returned to Paris dissatisfied and discouraged about the prospects for the peace settlement.

Unlike in Britain, there were no elections in France, and the Chamber of Deputies elected in 1914 remained until it had ratified the Treaty of Versailles. Election of a new Chamber by a new electoral system came only in November 1919. Meanwhile after a general debate on foreign policy, which was largely concerned with Bolshevik Russia, Clemenceau obtained a vote of confidence by 398 votes to 93. This gave him the authority to conduct the peace negotiations as he saw fit, without interference from the committees of the Chamber. Even Briand, who was intriguing against Clemenceau's conduct of affairs from behind the scenes throughout 1919, voted for him. In the course of his speech Clemenceau indicated clearly that he had not been carried away by the wave of enthusiasm for 'Wilsonism' that was temporarily sweeping France and indeed the whole of Europe. He declared that he would not give up his belief in the old system of alliances, and that it was vital that the four powers who had won the war should remain united.

He continued: *If some international guarantees on which light has not yet been shed, and which may be more difficult to establish in reality than in speeches and on paper, are offered in addition, I will willingly accept them. And if these supplementary guarantees allow us to reduce our military preparedness, I will do so with pleasure, for I would not wish to impose unnecessary burdens on my country. Only, I ask you to consider carefully. We are told: if you make a peace of justice, all will be easy. I ask you to look at a map of the world. There is no tribunal, whether that of Heaven or Hell to fix the borders of each state … The truth is that from the most remote depths of the historical past, peoples of the world have attacked each other to satisfy their own appetites and interests. Neither I nor you have made this history. It exists.*[13]

(Left to right) Clemenceau, President Wilson and Lloyd George on the day of the signing of the Treaty of Versailles, 28 June 1919.

II

The Paris Peace Conference

4

Opening of the Conference, January and February

The Peace Conference lasted from 18 January 1919 to 21 January 1920, although it was only in June and August 1920 that the treaties of Trianon with Hungary, and of Sèvres with the Ottoman Empire were signed. But by far the most important part was concerned with the Treaty of Versailles with Germany, signed on 28 June 1919. After that date Woodrow Wilson and Lloyd George left Paris, and the feeling that the destiny of the world was being decided there faded: the 13 subsequent months were concerned with detail. We are therefore really concerned with the six months from January to June 1919. They can be divided into four sections. In the first there are the opening weeks of the Conference when the term of a 'preliminary peace' was being employed. Apart from the public plenary sessions, the leading statesmen met as the Council of Ten; that is, the governmental heads and foreign ministers of the United States, Britain, France, Italy and Japan. Several commissions developed to deal with particular topics, above all that for the League of Nations to which President Wilson devoted most of his time. Except for drawing up the Covenant of the League, and disposing of Germany's colonies, little was decided at this stage. It was followed by a hiatus, when for different reasons the three chief protagonists were absent. This lasted from 8 February until 14 March; on 8 February Lloyd George went to Britain to deal with pressing issues at home, returning only on 5 March; Wilson was absent in the United States from 15 February until 14 March: Clemenceau was wounded in an attempted assassination on 19 February, and was out of action for several days. Although Clemenceau made a remarkably swift recovery, it was obvious that no serious progress could be made until both Lloyd George and Wilson had returned. So the third and crucial part of the conference was from Wilson's return on 14 March until the terms were presented to the German delegation on 7 May. In these two months Clemenceau, Lloyd George and Wilson met informally, and were able to reach decisions in a way that would have been impossible with the cumbersome procedures of the earlier period. At this stage the idea of a preliminary peace was tacitly abandoned. Their meetings are known as the Council of Four, as the Italian prime minister Vittorio Orlando was included; he played little part except to assert Italian claims, and indeed absented himself, as a protest against their partial rejection, for much of the time. The fourth stage, during which the Council of Four continued to meet and decide matters, and during which the German response to the original terms was considered, covers the period from 7 May to the signature of the Treaty of Versailles on 28 June.

The world leaders who were to negotiate the terms of the peace settlement assembled in Paris in the first days of January 1919, accompanied by hundreds of officials and temporary assistants, and by thousands of journalists. Clemenceau himself returned on 7 January from a week in the Vendée, where he had gone by night trains the last day of the year. He returned refreshed and invigorated: as he had told General Mordacq on his departure: *Every time in my life when I have felt down and a bit depressed, I have gone back to breathe the invigorating air of my birthplace, and nearly ever time I have returned rearmed and ready to continue the struggle.*[1]

He had stayed with some old friends, M and Mme Phillipon, at La Tranche, in a house right on the beach where he could enjoy the salt winds from the wintry sea. A few miles from this point he obtained the use of a tiny cottage, where he was to spend much of his time after his retirement, and which is now preserved as a Clemenceau museum. Mordacq tells us that he took no documents with him, and did not even read the newspapers. Instead he spent the week sightseeing in La Rochelle, Fontenay-le-Conte, La Roche-sur-Yon, and Luçon and other places familiar to him from his youth almost 70 years before.

On his return to Paris, on 7 January, he paid an informal visit to Colonel House, finding the latter engaged in discussion with the rest of the American delegation, including President Wilson, just returned from an excursion to Italy. House took Clemenceau into a separate room and had a long and emotional talk with him. House was convinced that he had for the first time persuaded Clemenceau that 'a League of Nations was for the best interests of France'. House's arguments, as he recounts them, seem very confused. On the one hand he accepted that now that Germany and Russia had disappeared as military powers, France remained the only great military power on the Continent. As England always sought to establish an equilibrium it 'would not look with favour upon the present situation'. Having established the likelihood of British hostility, House then asserted that the League of Nations plan would compel England and America to the aid of France in the event that another nation like Germany should try to crush it. 'The old tiger seemed to see it all and became enthusiastic. He placed both hands on my shoulders and said, *you are right. I am for the League of Nations as you have it in mind, and you may count upon me to work with you.*' According to House, after further discussion of the problems facing France in which Clemenceau was told that it was pure foolishness to think of cancellation of its war debt to the United States, the old man said to him, *I think of you as a brother and I want you to tell me everything that is in your mind, and we will work together just as if we were part of the same government*. In reality, there can be no doubt that Clemenceau's real views about the League were that it was a useless toy; if indulging the Americans in such matters gained their support for French interests where it mattered, he was happy to play along.[2]

The next day, 8 January, the Council of Ministers formally designated the French plenipotentiaries, Clemenceau himself, Pichon the Foreign Minister, André Tardieu, Louis Lucien Klotz, Minister of Finance, and the diplomat Jules Cambon, ambassador to Germany before the war. In reality only Tardieu was to play an important role. Known before 1914 as a brilliant new arrival on the political stage, now aged 43, he was Clemenceau's right-hand man throughout the negotiations. Having been High Commissioner in the United States from the time of American entry into the war he had good personal contacts with several American delegates.

Several political figures from the President of the Republic down, including Aristide Briand and Henri Franklin-Bouillon, felt that their claims to be part of the French negotiating team

THE FRENCH DELEGATION

The French plenipotentiaries, apart from Clemenceau, were:

Jules Cambon (1845–1935), one of two brothers who played a major role in diplomacy, his brother Paul being ambassador to Britain. Jules was ambassador to Germany from 1907–14; he was then made secretary general of the Foreign Office but was not involved in routine matters.

André Tardieu (1876–1945). A brilliant student, coming top in every competition, he began life as a journalist. Elected to Parliament in 1914, he served at the Front before going to the United States as High Commissioner in 1917. He was Clemenceau's principal assistant in 1919, and after the war was seen as his political heir. Although the dominant figure from 1928–32, his political career then faltered. He wrote several books on the need for constitutional reform, which had little influence.

Louis Loucheur (1872–1931). A successful entrepreneur in public works, he rose to prominence in public life with his immense contribution to the production of armaments, especially heavy artillery: at first assistant to the Minister of Munitions, Albert Thomas, he succeeded him as minister in September 1917, becoming Minister for Industrial Reconstruction in November 1918. He remained in politics after the war, associated with Briand and an advocate of reconciliation with Germany.

Louis Lucien Klotz (1868–1930). Finance Minister under Painlevé and Clemenceau, his role at the conference was limited to the issue of reparations. Even in this area he came to be marginalised, and Clemenceau paid more attention to Loucheur.

Stephen Pichon (1857–1933), entered politics as Clemenceau's protégé in 1885: discredited by the Panama scandal, he took up a diplomatic career, before returning to political life as Foreign Minister in Clemenceau's first government. Foreign Minister from 1917 to 1920, his part in events became extremely limited, as a result of ill-health.

had been unjustifiably ignored. But, with the support of his majority in Parliament, Clemenceau had a free hand to take his own decisions, and to consult whom he liked, whether plenipotentiaries or not. There would be no discussion of the details by Parliament, either in full session or in the committees of the Chamber and Senate. Poincaré would be informed to a minimal extent of the progress of negotiations, but not asked for his advice, much to his annoyance, recorded again and again in his diary. In flagrant disregard of the first of the Fourteen Points, diplomacy did not proceed in the public view. Nor did the professional diplomats themselves have much part to play. Lloyd George was contemptuous of the British Foreign Office and its officials, as Wilson was of his Secretary of State Robert Lansing and the State Department. In the French case Clemenceau was determined to control the vital decisions himself and to use advisors of his own choice, and the Foreign Minister, his protégé Stephen Pichon, was in no way an obstacle in his path.

Lloyd George and the British Dominion premiers arrived in Paris on 11 January: the next day informal meetings began at the Quai d'Orsay and on 16 January the armistice with Germany was renewed. Finally 18 January saw the first formal plenary session of the Peace Conference in the Foreign Minister's magnificent room in the Quai d'Orsay. This session emerged out of a meeting of the political leaders and their military advisors, continuing the series of wartime meetings known as the Supreme War Council. After some discussion of the renewal of the armistice, Lloyd George intervened, stating that he thought that the meeting had been called to discuss 'questions preliminary to the more formal Conferences on peace'. The military withdrew, and the meeting continued as the first plenary session of the Peace Conference. The terminology used by Lloyd George, of these meetings being a preliminary conference, to be followed, presumably, by another more formal and complete, remained in use until about March, when it was gradually dropped, and what had been the preliminary conference became the Peace Conference. This evolution from Supreme War Council to Peace Conference facilitated tacit acceptance of Clemenceau's chairmanship. This allowed Clemenceau to appoint Paul Dutasta as chief secretary, the official in charge of the whole administration of the Conference. There was some surprise at the appointment of Dutasta, who was an unknown figure: the rumour, certainly untrue, went around that he was Clemenceau's illegitimate son. In fact he was the son of a friend and associate of the Tiger, who was a businessman and important political contact in his Var constituency. Although unknown in Paris, the junior Dutasta had played an important role as ambassador to Switzerland during the war; in fact, in charge of intelligence services there. Clemenceau wasted this opportunity, as Dutasta did not have the ability to seize control of the complicated machinery that developed. Instead the British official Sir Maurice Hankey 'gradually and unobtrusively took charge, having the faculty of being able to put his hand on relevant documents ... without loss of time, so that M Clemenceau coming to depend on his as though he were actually Chief Secretary, would turn to him at intervals with the question *where is that bag of yours?*'[3]

The first period of the Conference from January to March was unsatisfactory and little progress was made. Apart from the formal plenary sessions it took the form of the Council of Ten and met virtually every day, with Clemenceau sitting in front of the fireplace, the interpreter Paul Mantoux to his right and Dutasta to his left. In addition many subcommittees were created, staffed in the main by official and the second-rank politicians. However, Woodrow Wilson insisted on attending the sessions of the League of Nations subcommittee.

Harold Nicolson has lucidly explained the disorganisation of this period of the Conference and its reasons. One was the decision to allow the smaller states to present their claims, territorial and otherwise, not only in writing, but orally. As well

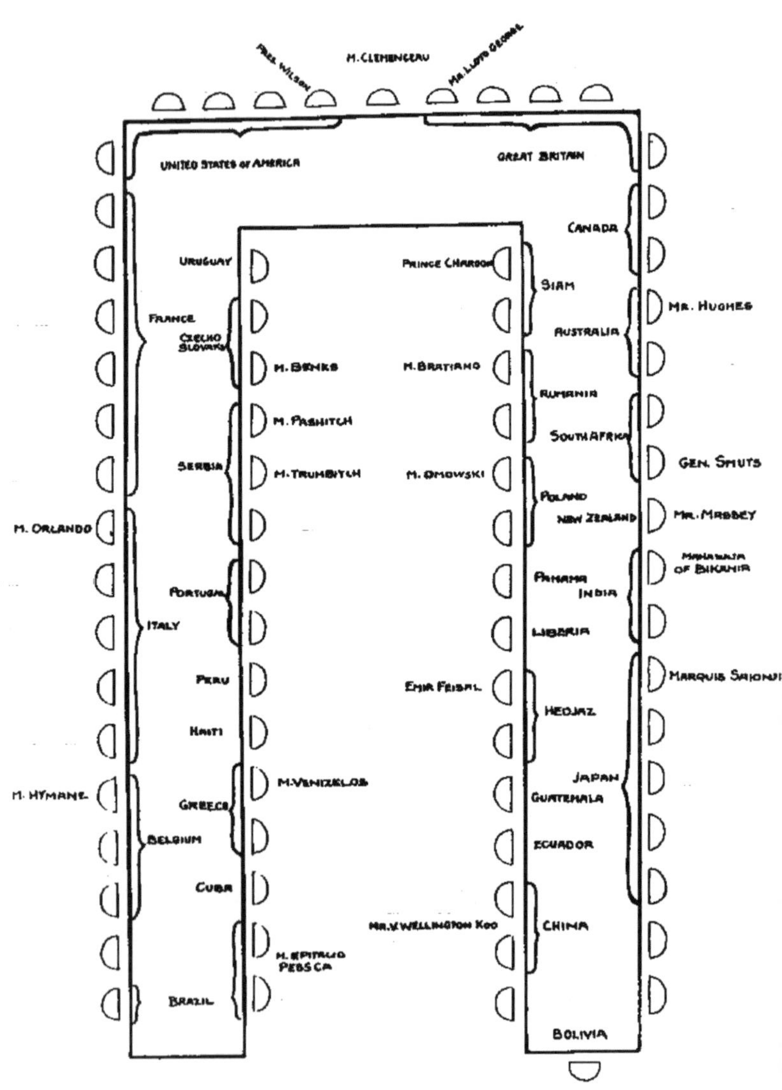

Sketch of the seating plan at the Paris Peace Conference.

as a serious waste of time this meant that the major questions concerning Germany and Austria were largely neglected, while the claims against them of the smaller powers were mixed up with their other claims against Hungary, Turkey and Bulgaria and with their mutual rivalries. Clemenceau and his appointee Dutasta must be held responsible for this slow progress. No doubt it was to some extent a deliberate tactic on Clemenceau's part. Poincaré noted in his diary for 24 February 1919 that Jules Cambon told him that Clemenceau had said to him before the Conference opened that he would leave the questions that interested France next to last; on the basis of what Clemenceau told him several times, Poincaré explained to Cambon that by indulging the Allies on these matters, Clemenceau hoped to win their support for what was essential to France: 'Alas by that he has ruined everything,' was Poincaré's verdict. But it is not evident that Clemenceau's tactics were as futile as Poincaré thought. In any case President Wilson was so determined to put the League of Nations before anything else that it was impossible to change this order of priorities.[4]

That anything at all was achieved in January and February owed much to Clemenceau's skill in handling the Council of Ten and the plenary sessions. His behaviour was very different in the two different bodies. In the Council of Ten, Lansing wrote, 'he showed patience and consideration towards his colleagues and seldom spoke until the others had expressed their views. He frequently spoke in English and curbed his sarcastic wit to avoid offending those whose support he needed. President Wilson, for example, was never in my presence a target for his sarcastic remarks.'[5] In the plenary sessions his manner was very different; he made it clear that the smaller powers were there to go through the formality of registering their approval.

Throughout the whole period of the negotiations Clemenceau conserved his strength by eschewing all distractions. He had no social life beyond briefing sessions with his assistants and the necessary intercourse with his political contacts. His daily routine had the following pattern. Waking and rising in the small hours he would breakfast on a peasant dish from the Vendée, half porridge, half stew, and spend several hours alone reading papers before his physical training instructor and masseur arrived for his daily exercise session. He would then depart by car to wherever his presence was required, returning home for a solitary lunch of boiled eggs. The afternoon and early evening would probably involve another session at the Conference or at somewhere related to domestic politics before he returned home for an early retirement to bed. This routine was possible because the distances involved were tiny. It was less that a kilometre from his flat on rue Franklin, near the Trocadéro, to the Quai d'Orsay with the Chamber of Deputies next door. A little further along the Boulevard St Germain brought him to his office at the Ministry of War in rue St Dominique. At this time the prime minister always held some other ministerial post, and there was no administrative infrastructure or geographical location for the premiership itself. A few hundred yards further east was the Senate in the Palais du Luxembourg, while the President of the Republic resided in the Elysée Palace on the other side of the Seine, but still within a few hundred yards. Clemenceau's rented flat where he had

'Plenary session at Quai d'Orsay at 3.15. Clemenceau rather high-handed with the smaller Powers. *Y a t il d'objections? Non? Adopté*. [Any objections? No ... Adopted] Like a machine gun.'
HAROLD NICOLSON[6]

lived since 1893 was extremely modest; it was a three-roomed apartment suitable for a minor official, although, being on the ground floor of its block, it had a garden. The Anglo-Saxon delegates to the conference were extremely impressed by the grandeur of the Quai d'Orsay and the other official buildings of the Republic, and still more by the Hall of Mirrors at Versailles when the time came for the signature of the Treaty, but such magnificence was certainly not reflected in the lifestyle of France's prime minister.

The first period of the Conference with its concentration on the League of Nations represented the highest degree of Anglo-American co-operation, to the complete exclusion of the French, along with the Italians and Japanese. The League of Nations Commission immediately decided to work on the basis of proposals (the Hurst-Miller draft) drafted by a British and an American expert. The French draft, based on work by Léon Bourgeois, who had coined the term Société des Nations, the French name eventually adopted for the League, in a book of 1908, was set aside. Bourgeois himself was virtually ignored in the subsequent discussion of the Commission. Bourgeois wanted the League to have its own army and general staff: as Germany was not to be a member, it amounted virtually to a continuation of the wartime alliance. The British and the Americans refused to contemplate this. In fact the only impact the French had on the design of the League was that their support for a Belgian proposal that the League Council should include representatives of the small powers, as well as the permanent Great Power members, led to its adoption. In all other respects French proposals were rejected or ignored. No doubt this was partly because Clemenceau took little interest in the matter. Bourgeois objected to the inclusion of a clause specifying the continued validity of the Monroe Doctrine. He pointed out the illogicality of this, but was defeated, and the amendment included. Clemenceau told the Americans that he was not interested and that Bourgeois and Larnaude were getting on his nerves.

The problem of Russia loomed in the background, but it turned out to be insoluble, and not much happened with regard to Russia that calls for detailed discussion. But it cannot pass without mention, as it was almost impossible for contemporaries to realise that what they saw as its temporary descent into revolutionary chaos would continue into the indefinite future. For France, Russia was the ally who, since 1893, had helped to counterbalance Germany, and it was hoped would do so again in the future. Not long before the fall of the Tsarist regime, in 1917, France and Russia had agreed to support each other's territorial claims against Germany in deals whose details were not revealed to Britain. From this point of view replacement of an understanding Russia with a naïve and critical United States was a major handicap for French negotiations in 1919. But the Russia of 1919, precariously and doubtfully under Bolshevik rule, could not be seen as a potential ally. French documents of the time normally referred to the new rulers of Russia as 'the Germano-Bolsheviks': Lenin in 1917 was seen as being simply a German agent, and Brockdorff-Rantzau's role in his journey through Germany back to Russia was not forgotten. As long as the Bolsheviks ruled Russia it was assumed that they would remain under German influence, and that an essential element of the European balance of power would not be restored. For these reasons Allied intervention in the Russian Civil War, which had begun in 1918 in the vain hope of recreating an eastern front against Germany, was allowed to drift on until the autumn of 1919 and even afterwards. A small number of

French troops had even landed in Odessa after the armistice, in December 1918, in the hope of preventing the Ukraine and southern Russia from falling under Bolshevik control when the German and Austrian occupying armies withdrew. The Allies hoped that with minimal military help the White (anti-Bolshevik) Russians would win the Civil War, thus allowing the eventual reestablishment of a Russian state that would be independent of Germany.

The subject of Allied intervention in the Russian Civil War has provoked substantial historical literature, which for the most part is not relevant to this study.[7] But the abortive discussions of what to do about Russia need to be mentioned. President Wilson, although he had allowed American troops to be committed to Russia in 1918 was less firm in his abhorrence of the Bolsheviks than the prevailing opinion in France and Britain. Indeed the sixth of the Fourteen Points was an almost unintelligible effusion about Russia, demanding 'the best and freest co-operation of the other nations of the world in obtaining for her an unhampered and unembarrassed opportunity for the independent determination of her own political development and national policy'.

In early January 1919, when the wave of messianic Wilsonism was sweeping the civilised world, it seemed impossible to exclude Russia from the crowds of suitors and supplicants congregating in Paris. The Whites already had representatives in Paris claiming to speak for Russia, known as the Russian Political Conference. But as the Bolsheviks controlled the heartland of the Russian Empire, it would have been absurd to simply accept the self-appointed spokesmen of their opponents. Lloyd George, with Wilson's support, proposed that representatives of all the parties at war in Russia be invited to take part in the conference, provided that they agreed to abandon their hostilities. Clemenceau vetoed this idea by refusing to accept a Bolshevik delegation in Paris. So Wilson then proposed that the Russian representatives should be invited to meet each other and Allied delegates at some other place, in fact the island of Prinkipo in the Sea of Marmara, which could be reached from Russia without crossing any third country. There was to be a truce in Russia, and the meeting was to begin on 15 February. This proposal came to nothing, being rejected by both sides: the news of this rejection reached Paris on 12 February, sparking further discussion of Russian affairs at a meeting of the Council of Ten on 14 February, just before Wilson's departure for the United States.

The first period of the Peace Conference negotiations virtually came to an end with the adoption of the draft Covenant of the League of Nations on 14 February 1919 at the third plenary session. Wilson set sail for the United States the next day, only returning on 14 March. As Lloyd George had already left for London on 8 February, it was obvious that no major decisions could be taken before their return. And then Clemenceau himself was put out of action by the assassination attempt of 19 February. After this hiatus the conference resumed in a very different manner with the Council of Four replacing the Council of Ten.

5 The Pause: February to March

This chapter covers the period from 15 February to 24 March. At first there was a pause in the negotiations, caused in the first place by the absence of President Wilson, and of Lloyd George. With Wilson's return on 14 March events began to move with greater rapidity, but it is only from 24 March that we have the full record of proceedings in the Council of Four provided by the interpreter Paul Mantoux's notes.

With both Lloyd George and Woodrow Wilson absent, no progress could be made on the major question facing the Allies, the peace terms to be offered to Germany. During this period each participant formulated their desiderata more precisely, seeking to prepare for the hard negotiations needed before they could present a common front to Germany. It was obvious that matters could not continue as they had been under the system of January and February, with the Council of Ten and all its subcommittees and investigating groups, if terms were to be presented to Germany within a reasonable timescale. When Lloyd George, Wilson and Clemenceau were all back in action in Paris, that is from 14 March, there began a series of informal meetings among the top leaders and their closest advisors that evolved into what was called the Council of Four. Besides the imperative of drawing-up terms to present to Germany the need for rapid decision was underlined by the growth of social unrest. The high point for this unrest was March and April. As well as what turned out in the end to be limited strikes and protests in the victor states, Britain and France, these two months saw unrest in eastern and central Europe that could be interpreted as the westward march of Bolshevism from its base in Moscow. In Germany there was a general strike and violent unrest in Berlin, and the 'Soviet republic' in Munich, only crushed with much bloodshed on 2 May. On 22 March the moderate Mihály Károlyi resigned in Hungary and was replaced by the Communist Bela Kun. In Russia itself where hopes and fears see-sawed violently throughout 1919, March and April saw Bolshevik advances.

Thus by the second half of March there was a sense of urgency among the peacemakers that produced the Council of Four and a new insistence on getting to grips with the most important questions. But that could only come about when the 'Big Three' were all back in Paris and able to confer together. In fact the hiatus can be said to continue until Lloyd George took some of his closest advisors for a weekend of reflection at Fontainebleau. The resulting 'Fontainebleau memorandum,' warning of the danger of presenting Germany with too harsh terms, in a sense cleared the air for the hard bargaining that followed. Although every question had implications for all the others, and the discussion in the Council of Four mixed everything together, they will be separated in the two following chapters, one dealing with territorial matters, the other with reparations.

When Wilson departed he gave Lansing strict instructions to follow the line of conduct that he had himself laid down.

As he had not yet committed himself in any precise way this meant that Lansing had no authority to decide anything at all about the future terms of peace. The immediate business of the Supreme Council was to deal with the third and final renewal of the armistice with Germany, which was accomplished on 16 February. Much to the annoyance of the French, this involved a relaxation of the economic blockade, which had been continued up to this time as a means of maintaining pressure on the enemy. On the other hand the Germans were forced to desist from attacking the Poles in Posen and Upper Silesia.

The next three days, 15 to 17 February, were spent discussing the Russian situation. This had come to the agenda because 15 February was the deadline that had been set for replies to the proposed meeting at Prinkipo of the different parties involved in the Russian Civil War. The reply from the Whites was an outright refusal: that from Lenin equivocated. They were hurriedly discussed on the afternoon of 14 February before Wilson's departure, but there was no time for a decision before he left to catch his boat train. The President's unhelpful advice was that he would like all Allied troops to be withdrawn from Russia at once, but that he would accept the decision of the Council when it had heard the British proposal.

The next day began with a paper from General Alby, the French chief of staff, outlining the situation in Russia; paradoxically, Alby presented a picture of Bolshevik advance and White defeat while arguing that a very small contribution of military aid on the part of the Allies would be enough to turn the tide. Winston Churchill had been sent over by Lloyd George, detained in London to deal with a looming strike in the coalfields and general labour unrest, to present the views of the British cabinet. Secretary of State for War and Air since January 1919, Churchill was not involved in the peace negotiations themselves, but devoted himself to planning the overthrow of Bolshevism in Russia. As on so many things, Lloyd George himself equivocated, allowing Churchill to develop ambitious plans and then torpedoing them, as on this occasion. Churchill produced an apocalyptic vision of Germany dominating a Bolshevik Russia that would produce 'a predatory confederation stretching from the Rhine to Yokohama menacing the vital interests of the British Empire in India and elsewhere, menacing indeed the future of the world'.[1] To prevent this, the Allies had to strengthen the anti-Bolshevik forces in Russia, so as to overthrow the latter who were German puppets.

Before the Council of Ten could come to any decision Churchill found the ground cut from under his feet by Lloyd George whom he had informed of his proposals. Lloyd George replied; 'Am very alarmed at your second telegram about planning war against the Bolsheviks. The cabinet have never authorised any such proposal … An expensive war of aggression against Russia is the way to strengthen Bolshevism in Russia and create it at home.' Lloyd George got his private secretary Philip Kerr to show this telegram to House and to Balfour, thus completely undermining Churchill's authority. This led to a discussion on the afternoon of 17 February that was so acrimonious that it was excluded from the minutes. It appears that Clemenceau and Sonnino supported Churchill, while House and Balfour objected strenuously. Clemenceau made a particularly offensive speech for which he later apologised. Finally it was agreed that the military advisors should continue to study the situation, reporting not jointly to the Council but each to his own nation's political authorities.

General Sir Henry Wilson wrote in his diary: 'the greatest depth of impotence I have seen the Frocks fall to.' Attempts to produce an agreed policy on Russia were abandoned. On 4 March Britain decided to withdraw its troops from Russia. On 27 March the French decided to withdraw from Odessa.[2]

Clemenceau had said that he wanted to devote 19 February to consideration of the Russian question, but it turned out to be the day he was shot in an assassination attempt. The shots were fired at 8.40 a.m. as Clemenceau was being driven by car from his flat in rue Franklin to his office at the Ministry of War. The car had only gone a few yards and was moving slowly as it turned from rue Franklin to Boulevard Delessert. Cottin, the would-be assassin had been hiding behind a Vespasienne, a primitive urinal by the kerb, from where he emerged to fire several shots, hitting Clemenceau once; the bullet lodged in his shoulder blade and the doctors decided not to try to remove it. *They decided I needed some lead for ballast*, he joked, one of many jokes that he made about the wounding. His car turned round to bring him straight back to his own apartment where Drs Tuffier and Gosset arrived rapidly. He greeted the latter by saying, *What a pity that he missed me, it would have been a magnificent apotheosis*.[3]

Cottin was set upon by a crowd of passers-by and might have been lynched if he had not been saved by the police. He is usually called an anarchist, but he seems to have been a disturbed individual with no links to any organised political group. He was tried and sentenced within a few weeks: his victim, who had always opposed the death penalty, insisted that there could be no question of its application and Cottin was given a long prison term. Clemenceau was, however, less pleased when Cottin was released after only four years in gaol by the left-wing government that came to power in 1924. The

Left argued, with what might seem a strange logic, that there was an unfair comparison between the judicial fates of Cottin and of Villain who had assassinated Jaurès in 1914. Villain had been left in prison for four years, and then was tried and acquitted by a perverse jury verdict, a few days after Cottin was found guilty. Clemenceau made an astonishingly rapid recovery from what was without doubt a dangerous wound for a man of his age. He claimed that it was due to his physical fitness, telling his colleague Senator Doumergue, that *If I had carried your weight, I would have had it*. To which Doumergue, aged 56 to Clemenceau's 78 replied, 'Don't worry; it will happen to you when you get old.'[4]

He was nursed in his own bedroom by a nun, Sister Théonaste, who had previously looked after him after he had had his prostate removed. As on the previous occasion he teased her mercilessly, pitting his atheism against her religious faith. He said to Mordacq, while sister Théonaste was dressing his wound, that he was in a quandary, because while his recovery was dependent on her prayers to the eternal being, he had already convinced her that the Devil did not exist, and that with a few more days in his company, she might be convinced that God did not exist either; and *then, what would happen?*[5] But in the meantime she was the only authority he would accept on the subject of what he could and could not do. After a couple of days during which he saw only Mordacq, Mandel and his family, he began to resume his work, asking House to come to see him in his flat on 22 February. The meeting was only for 20 minutes. House noted: 'The poor fellow has not been able to leave his chair since he was shot … He should not be permitted to see visitors'.[6]

Nevertheless Clemenceau presented House with the points that he saw as vital in the territorial settlement. As House reported by cable to Wilson: 'He is insistent upon the creation of a Rhenish Republic. There will be about four million Germans aggregated in this way. He desires that this Republic should be exempt from any indemnity: that they should have no armed force: that everything should be done to make them prosperous and contented, so that they will not want to join the German federation, and if they have such a desire they will not be permitted to do so. He continued by saying that Danzig should go to Poland, and that Austria should not be permitted to join the German federation'.[7] In spite of his insistence that a Rhineland separate from Germany was essential for French security, Clemenceau was equally determined to maintain the alliance with Britain and the United States. His problem was how to combine these two incompatible aims. Every spokesman for Britain and America had rejected the idea of a separate Rhineland from its first proposal by Foch at the end of 1918. On 27 February he returned to his office at the Ministry of War in the morning and to the meeting of the Council of Ten in the afternoon.

A working group of Tardieu, Edward Mezes and Kerr met on 11–12 March in a vain attempt to resolve the deadlock. Mezes hardly spoke. Tardieu says that he had eight hours of dialogue with Kerr, Lloyd George's faithful spokesman. Tardieu and Kerr decided that they could make no progress, and that the issue must be passed to their leaders. Lloyd George had already floated the idea of an Anglo-American guarantee to France against unprovoked German aggression at the British cabinet meeting of 4 March, and on 12 March he told House of this, without contacting the French.[8]

On 14 March, Wilson arrived back in Paris. Waiting for him at the station, Clemenceau had an interesting conversation with Poincaré, recorded in the latter's diary: 'Today

Clemenceau is *angry* with the English, and especially with Lloyd George. *I won't budge*, he said *I will act like a hedgehog and wait until they come to talk to me. I will yield nothing. We will see if they can manage without me. Lloyd George is a trickster. He has managed to turn me into a 'Syrian' ... I don't like being double-crossed. Lloyd George has deceived me. He made me the finest promises, and now he breaks them. Fortunately I think that at the moment we can count on American support. What is the worst of all, is that the day before yesterday, Lloyd George said to me, 'Well, now that we are going to disarm Germany, you no longer need the Rhine.'* I said to Clemenceau: 'Does disarmament then seem to him to give the same guarantees? Does he think that, in the future, we can be sure of preventing Germany from rebuilding her army?' *We are in complete agreement*, said Clemenceau: *it is a point I will not yield.*'[9]

The same afternoon, 14 March, Clemenceau met Lloyd George and Wilson at the American delegation's quarters in the Hotel Crillon. They had a two-hour meeting without secretaries or interpreters, in which the French premier presented once again all the arguments for the separation of the Rhineland from Germany, and met with the same resistance from the Anglo-Saxons. Then, without him asking for it, as he later told the Senate, the guarantee was offered, but with the counterpart that any idea of a buffer state or of military occupation should be abandoned. This offer placed Clemenceau in a difficult position. He did not want to reject the offer of the Anglo-American guarantee, but he still felt that French security demanded much more. After consulting with Tardieu, Loucheur and Pichon, he decided to accept the offer of the guarantee, but to continue pressing for demilitarisation of the left bank and its occupation with bridgeheads across the river at Mainz, Koblenz and Koln. He also demanded the 1814 frontier for Alsace, not the reduced area allotted in 1815, with an extension beyond to include the coal basin of the Saar. These French demands were presented in a memorandum of 17 March. It did, however, by implication, make an important concession. There was no more talk of a Rhineland *state* or *states*. The future political status of the Rhineland was not mentioned. This meant that it would remain under German sovereignty. Clemenceau thought that demilitarisation would provide security for France without vain metaphysical debates over sovereignty. The German reoccupation of the Rhineland in 1936 proved him wrong on this point. If the Rhineland had been a separate buffer state, it would not have been so easy to dismiss the reoccupation as 'Hitler going into his own backyard'.[10] Throughout March the leaders inched towards a compromise, the main lines of which were that a separate Rhineland state was dropped and a temporary Allied military occupation was agreed. 'Temporary' for the French meant 30 years or longer, while Lloyd George was hoping for a few months: Wilson did not seem much concerned.

They found themselves at loggerheads not only on the Rhineland question but also on the related topic of the Saar, and on the Ottoman Empire and reparations. It was at this time that Clemenceau and Lloyd George almost came to blows over Syria. Poincaré tells us that Clemenceau regarded the territorial questions as more important than reparations, and was prepared to use them as a bargaining counter. On 23 March Poincaré recorded in his diary: 'A few days ago Clemenceau, wishing to subordinate everything to a French success on the territorial questions, said to Loucheur: *be conciliatory on financial questions. Study ways of giving some satisfaction in England, even on the question of priority …*' but in view of Lloyd George's latest attitude on territorial questions, Clemenceau told Loucheur to be more resistant.

We must do everything we can to be just towards the Germans: but persuading them that we have been just towards them is another matter. I believe that we can arrange things so that the world is spared further German aggression for a long time, but the German mentality will not be changed soon … Take note that no one in Germany distinguishes between the just and unjust demands of the Allies …

CLEMENCEAU IN THE COUNCIL OF FOUR, 27 MARCH 1919.[12]

Lloyd George and his chief advisors, Sir Henry Wilson, Hankey and Kerr, spent the weekend of 22–23 March away from the hectic atmosphere in Paris at Fontainebleau, returning with a memorandum to be presented to the other Allies on 25 March. This document was aimed at the French, and argued that if Germany were treated too harshly it would 'throw in her lot with Bolshevism, and place her resources, her brains, her vast organising power at the disposal of the revolutionary fanatics'.[11]

The precise proposals made in the Fontainebleau memorandum included the following:

(i) The demilitarisation of the Rhineland, but no occupation.
(ii) The 1814 frontier for the Saar, or French right to obtain coal for ten years.
(iii) A Polish corridor to Danzig that would include the smallest possible number of Germans.

Clemenceau's reply accused Lloyd George of demanding the utmost concessions from Germany in everything that directly involved British interests, and then seeking to appease it at the expense of France. He claimed that this would not even satisfy Germany, as it was concerned above all with its overseas ambitions: *The note suggests that moderate territorial conditions should be imposed on Germany in Europe in order not to leave a profound feeling of resentment after peace. This method might have value, if the late war had been for Germany a European war. This, however, was not the case. Before the war Germany was a great naval power whose future lay upon the water. This world power was Germany's pride: she will not console herself for having lost it … If it is necessary to appease her she should be offered colonial satisfaction, naval expansion, or satisfaction with regard to her commercial expansion.*[13]

As for the danger of Bolshevism, Clemenceau stated that Lloyd George's proposals would lead to Bolshevism in France and in the Eastern European states. Lloyd George returned an even more bitter reply, which he did not expect to be taken very seriously. The memorandum was discussed by the Council of Four on 27 March, and was then dropped. But this discussion showed its protagonists the wide gap between their respective positions. It certainly would not be correct to state the difference as being between France insisting on a harsh treaty and Lloyd George pleading for a moderate one. Clemenceau was surely correct in his view that Lloyd George demanded harsh terms in everything that concerned Britain, while seeking to limit what France saw as its essential safeguards

It could be argued also, that Lloyd George insisted on the clauses that provoked the most anger and resentment in German opinion without being of practical importance for future security; then, having written them into the Treaty, within a few weeks he began to backtrack about their application, encouraging German resistance. This can be seen in the topic of punishing German war criminals from the Kaiser downwards. Although Clemenceau certainly did not oppose this idea, it was Lloyd George who pressed for it most vociferously and publicly, until the signature of the Treaty. Very soon afterwards British policy turned away from serious attempts to enforce these clauses, while France and Belgium persisted in putting on trial German perpetrators of war crimes, in person or *in absentia*. Two different issues become intertwined here. One was the attempt to try relatively subordinate figures who had committed specific offences, such as executing prisoners and civilians. The other was the attempt to satisfy public opinion by indicting the German leadership from the Kaiser and the Crown Prince down. The slogan 'Hang the Kaiser' emerged in the British election of 1918, and never had the same resonance in France. This is not to say that French opinion would have opposed it, and Clemenceau supported Lloyd George's idea of putting the Kaiser on trial. But for him, and for French opinion in general, specific crimes committed by lower-level figures were more important. It was at the beginning of April 1919, at the height of the conflict over almost all aspects of the Treaty, that the British and French got Wilson to agree to what became Article 227 calling for the trial of 'William II of Hohenzollern, formerly German Emperor, for a supreme offence against international morality and the sanctity of treaties'.[14] This and the next three clauses providing for the trial of German war criminals provoked the last-ditch resistance of the German government to signature of the Treaty; only when his military advisor, General Groener, told President Ebert that there was no possibility of military resistance, did the government agree to sign.

At that point Lloyd George was so enthusiastic that he got Clemenceau to agree that the trial of the Kaiser should take place in Britain. But as soon as August, British policy began to vacillate. The Dutch, who would have had to agree to the extradition of the ex-Kaiser, were getting hints that the Allies were not serious in their demands. When Clemenceau, as one of his last official acts, then sent the formal Allied demand for extradition, it was clear that nothing would happen. By this time the procedures that had been set in motion for the arrest of subordinate German war criminals had produced a list of 854 names beginning with Hindenburg. Lloyd George was horrified at the number and eminence of those on the list, and tried to get it reduced, but Clemenceau told him that French opinion would not allow him to agree.[15] A month later his successor as prime minister, Alexandre Millerand, agreed to the British idea that the trials should take place in Germany. There followed a complete fiasco from the Allied point of view. The few trials that did take place resulted in acquittals in the face of the evidence, or very light sentences. The accused were seen as national heroes by German opinion. Thus, an Allied commission decided in January 1922 to return to the policy of enforcing Articles 228 to 230 of the Treaty by conducting trials themselves. This led to a series of trials before French and Belgian courts in the face of British criticism, until the fall of Poincaré brought them to an end. The most unfortunate result of these developments was that opinion in Britain, and in the United States, became convinced that accounts of German war crimes were simply, as the Germans themselves claimed, false Allied propaganda. In reality, as has recently been rediscovered and pointed out by meticulous research, German atrocities, especially those involving the execution of innocent civilians including women and children, in the first weeks of the war, were real and unprecedented in modern European warfare.[16] However, so successful was the German campaign of denial that rejection of the 'atrocities' of 1914 served in its turn to make British opinion reluctant to accept the truth about German atrocities in the Second World War, including genocide.

6

The German Frontiers and Treaties of Guarantee

Lloyd George came back from Britain convinced that the discussions of the Council of Ten had to be ended, and that they must be replaced by meetings of the heads of government to achieve more rapid decision-making. Neither Wilson nor Clemenceau objected and they began to meet informally soon after Wilson's return to Paris on 14 March. These meetings evolved into the Council of Four from 24 March, while the Council of Ten atrophied, and ceased to meet after another week, being replaced by the Council of Five, that is the foreign ministers alone. In fact from this point the important negotiations took place in the Council of Four. In reality for lengthy periods there were three, as the Italian premier Orlando was absent in protest from 21 April to 6 May, and again in late May and at the end of June when he fell from office. Handicapped by his lack of knowledge of English, he had taken little part in the discussions, and, in any case, Italy was concerned above all with its own territorial claims which did not relate to Germany. So in fact the Council of Four meant the deliberations of President Wilson, Lloyd George and Clemenceau, with House replacing Wilson from 3 to 8 April, because of the latter's illness. Meetings were normally at Wilson's residence, although occasionally elsewhere, at Lloyd George's apartment or in Clemenceau's room at the Ministry of War. At first there was no provision for secretarial records, but from 15 April Hankey attended and produced brief minutes and recorded decisions. However there was still no formally prepared agenda, and different topics were discussed in an almost random fashion. This chapter will cover discussions about the German frontiers, German disarmament and the Anglo-American guarantees to France, while the next chapter will deal with reparations. It must be remembered, however, that all of these key questions were interrelated, which is why in reality the three statesmen discussed them simultaneously.

Before March 1919 there had been no serious discussion of these vital matters by the three principal figures. Fixing German frontiers involved the following: the return of Alsace-Lorraine, annexed in 1871 from Germany to France, the Saarland, rectification of the German-Belgian and German-Danish frontiers, and Germany's Eastern Frontier with Poland. The attribution of Germany's overseas colonies had already been decided in connection with the League of Nations and mandates in the first few weeks of the negotiations. Although this had produced serious confrontation, above all between Woodrow Wilson and the Australian prime minister, William Hughes, Clemenceau and France were scarcely involved in this. German colonial territory in equatorial Africa was divided between Britain and France, without any of the bad feeling that arose over their relative shares of the Ottoman Empire, and the Council of Four had nothing further to say on this matter. Ceding of German territory to

Belgium and Denmark does not need discussion here, as it involved little conflict among the victors. These questions were settled by the lower level negotiators. In the case of the areas of Schleswig given to Denmark the relatively simple linguistic frontier allowed a plebiscite to produce a clear-cut result, acceptable to both sides. If only national frontiers in other parts of Europe could have been resolved in such a straightforward manner.

Nor was there discussion of the principle of the return of Alsace-Lorraine to France, which after all had been one of Wilson's Fourteen Points. However, the details soon proved to be more troublesome, as the northern frontier of Alsace had varied over the years. A simple return of the territory annexed in 1871 would give France the frontier of 1815. But France demanded the frontier proposed in 1814, before Napoleon's last throw of the dice, which was further north, reaching into the Saar basin. If France were to be granted the frontier of 1792 the line would be even further north. Even that line though, would not bring the whole of the Saar coalfield into France, which was what was needed. France had been handicapped throughout the previous century by its limited coal resources. Coal was the vital ingredient in the 19th-century industrial revolution, and still seemed essential in 1919 if France was to be a major industrial state in the future. In the immediate term its need for coal was desperate. A large part of the coal that France had had in 1914 was mined in the area that had been behind the German lines. When they retreated in the last weeks of the war, the Germans had sabotaged as much as they could, and it was accepted by all concerned that for the next few years Germany should be forced to make good the energy deficit resulting from its activities. But France wanted more than this short-term fix. A major shift in the economic balance between herself and Germany was an important aim of policy. This needed long-term control of the Saar coal basin, which was fought for by Clemenceau in his negotiations with Wilson and Lloyd George. Another French aspiration was to use the iron ore field of Lorraine to put France ahead of Germany as a producer of iron and steel.

Iron and steel production, of course, meant using vast amounts of coal in the smelting process, but the coal of the Saar was not suitable for that use, and so the conflict over the Saar was not directly relevant to this question, which has been much discussed in recent French historical literature. But in the immediate post-war years, the Saar's coal was vital for the general economic life of France. Unfortunately annexation of the Saarland meant head-on conflict with the principle of national self-determination. As Lloyd George put it, he did not want to create a new Alsace-Lorraine, replicating the lost provinces so mourned by France between 1871 and 1918.

So the Saar became one of the first matters to be discussed in the Council of Four with considerable acrimony. At the second meeting on 28 March, after a morning session with Keynes and Klotz about reparations, Tardieu presented a memorandum presenting the French demands. The maximum he wanted included the whole of the Saar basin: the minimum was the frontier of 1814 and provision for French control of the coalmines beyond that line. Neither Wilson nor Lloyd George could accept either of these, although Wilson's opposition was much more determined than that of Lloyd George. The latter at once, on 28 March, proposed as a compromise, a neutral Saar, detached from Germany, autonomous but under French suzerainty. This was not far from the maximum French demand, but it was rejected by Wilson, who argued for the Saar remaining German, but with a guarantee that it would temporarily supply coal to France. The French argued that not only did they need the coal, but that many of the inhabitants were, in any case, French, or at least would be happy to become French. Their case involved looking back to the historically dubious welcome the area was supposed to have given to French invaders in 1792, so that if the inhabitants now felt themselves German it was because of a century of Germanisation, since the Saar had been assigned to Prussia in 1815.

In spite of his initial objections Wilson was worn down in two weeks of intense argument in the Council of Four, backed up by similar debate in a sub-committee where Tardieu met the official advisors, Charles H Haskins (USA) and James Headlam-Morley (Britain). The crucial meetings of the Council of Four were on 9–10 April, when the main lines of the eventual settlement emerged. The Saar was to be detached from Germany and to be an autonomous state administered by the League of Nations for a period of 15 years, during which France was to own the coalmines. At the end of that period a plebiscite would be held in which the inhabitants would be asked it they wished to continue the *status quo* or to unite with Germany or with France. Thus France would control the Saar coalmines for at least 15 years, and have the chance to prove the contention that the Saarlanders were or could become non-German. In fact, in 1935 they voted overwhelmingly to rejoin Germany in spite of the fact that it meant a largely working class and Socialist community voting to join Hitler's Germany. It was due to Wilson's resistance, rather than any strong stance on the part of Lloyd George, that this compromise was imposed on Clemenceau.[1]

North and east of the Saar one comes to the much larger area of the Rhineland, as the area was known in the 1919 discussions. The Rhineland, the left bank of the Rhine from Alsace to the Dutch frontier, with bridgeheads on the right bank, was seen by the French as essential for their future security. In this case it was not because of its economic resources such as the coal of the Saar, but because of its strategic importance. A German invasion of France would have to be launched from and through the Rhineland, and thus French control of it was required. Again, as in the case of the Saar, after bitter argument between the three victors, a compromise was hammered out, some of the main lines being remarkably similar. In both cases the French demand for a permanent autonomous state was rejected in favour of a 15-year period of Allied control, although the demilitarisation of the Rhineland was without time limit.

France had been putting its plans for the Rhineland to its allies since soon after the armistice, but had not met with any response until the issue came before the Council of Four. In fact Foch's insistence on the occupation of the Rhineland, endorsed by Clemenceau as part of the armistice terms already foreshadowed later policy on the question. Foch followed this with a memorandum of 27 November 1918 in which he argued for the complete separation of the Rhineland from Germany and its transformation into an independent state whose neutrality would be guaranteed by the Great Powers. Somewhat inconsistent with the proposed neutrality was the idea that an army raised in the Rhineland would help to correct the demographic imbalance between Germany and France. Lord Derby, the British ambassador, reported on Foch's scheme to Arthur Balfour, the British Foreign Secretary, on 14 December 1918, stating that Clemenceau had vetoed the part of the scheme involving a Rhineland army. Nevertheless Foch was allowed to present his Rhineland scheme to Lloyd George when he visited London with Clemenceau between 30 November and 3 December 1918. Clemenceau had to manoeuvre carefully to keep control of vital decisions, such as those about the future status of the Rhineland, in his own hands. When Bonar Law told him that a British general would be dismissed in ten minutes if he adopted Foch's insubordinate attitude, Clemenceau replied that the political situation in France did not allow him that luxury. Foch had powerful friends and the support of wide strands of public opinion. Foch's plan for the Rhineland was formally presented to the British and the Americans in a note of 10 January 1919. The Rhineland was to be detached from German sovereignty and to be 'autonomous', but incorporated into a permanent military alliance with France, Belgium and Luxembourg, itself allied with Britain. In fact this meant the Rhineland becoming a French puppet state.[2]

There was no chance of Foch's plans being accepted by either Britain or the United States, and Clemenceau never committed himself to them in their entirety. He supported the idea of an independent Rhineland state, prohibited from rejoining Germany whatever the wishes of the inhabitants, but without Foch's idea of incorporating it in an Allied military system. He argued for this version in a meeting with House on 22 February, and it was presented formally on 25 February in a memorandum drafted by Tardieu. This stressed that the western frontier of Germany should be the Rhine, but that France had no territorial ambitions on the left bank. The French case was that only an Allied occupation of the Rhineland could give France the military security that Britain and the United States derived from their naval power. It has been argued by H I Nelson that Clemenceau and Tardieu made these demands as a bargaining position, an extreme stance from which they could retreat in return for concessions. For, as Clemenceau never ceased to assert, his overriding concern was to maintain the alliance with the Anglo-Saxons. Only by arguing first for a Rhineland buffer state could he turn to his right-wing critics, led by Foch and Poincaré, and tell them that he had been forced to abandon that claim to maintain Allied unity.

No progress was made on the Rhineland question until after the hiatus caused by the absence of Lloyd George and Wilson, and the assassination attempt on Clemenceau. Talks at the lower level between Tardieu, Philip Kerr and the American advisor Dr Mezes on 11–12 March were deadlocked. However, discussion of the clauses of the Treaty relating to the disarmament of Germany had made progress, and almost simultaneously arrived at agreement on provisions relating to the Rhineland. On 10 March the Council of Ten, with Lloyd George, Balfour, Clemenceau, Lansing and House all present, agreed that the left bank of the Rhine be demilitarised: 'That is to say, the inhabitants of this territory will not be permitted to bear arms or receive any military training … and no fortifications, depots, establishments, railway constructions or works of any kind adapted to military purposes will be permitted to exist within the area.' Thus a demilitarised buffer zone, if not a buffer state was agreed to. By this time Clemenceau had become thoroughly disillusioned with Lloyd George, complaining to Loucheur and to House that *Lloyd George had broken his word over the Rhineland, Syria and the division of Reparations.*[3]

Lloyd George had broken his word over the Rhineland, Syria and the division of Reparations.
CLEMENCEAU

Unaware of Clemenceau's anger, it was at this point that

Lloyd George decided on the idea of a joint Anglo-American guarantee against unprovoked German aggression, as an alternative to the buffer state. For him, it would also serve the purpose of binding the United States into a European security system. Lloyd George met Wilson immediately after the ceremonial arrival, and the two men agreed rapidly, in fact casually, on the treaty of guarantee. It was offered to Clemenceau that afternoon. He asked for time to consider, and discussed it with Pichon, Loucheur and Tardieu over the next three days. On 17 March a French memorandum delivered their reply, arguing that the treaties of guarantee were not enough to give France security without other measures. The French did agree to drop their demand for political separation of the Rhineland from Germany, but insisted on stringent conditions to enforce demilitarisation of the area.

Over the next month the details of the Rhineland clauses of the Treaty were argued over between the three principals and their advisors, in counterpoint with their other conflicts over the Saar, reparations and the German-Polish frontier. By the end of April, they had managed to agree on the terms to be presented to the Germans. The Rhineland was to be demilitarised with no time limit. It was to be occupied by the Allied armies for up to 15 years; that is, it was divided into three zones, one to be occupied for 15 years, one for ten years, and one for five. There were, however, two other provisions, one allowing for earlier evacuation if the Germans were seen to have fulfilled the terms of the Treaty, the other allowing for the occupation to continue after the 15 years if the terms had not been carried out. These clauses well illustrated the different views of British and French: while the British had only reluctantly accepted the military occupation and hoped that it could be ended in months, the French could argue

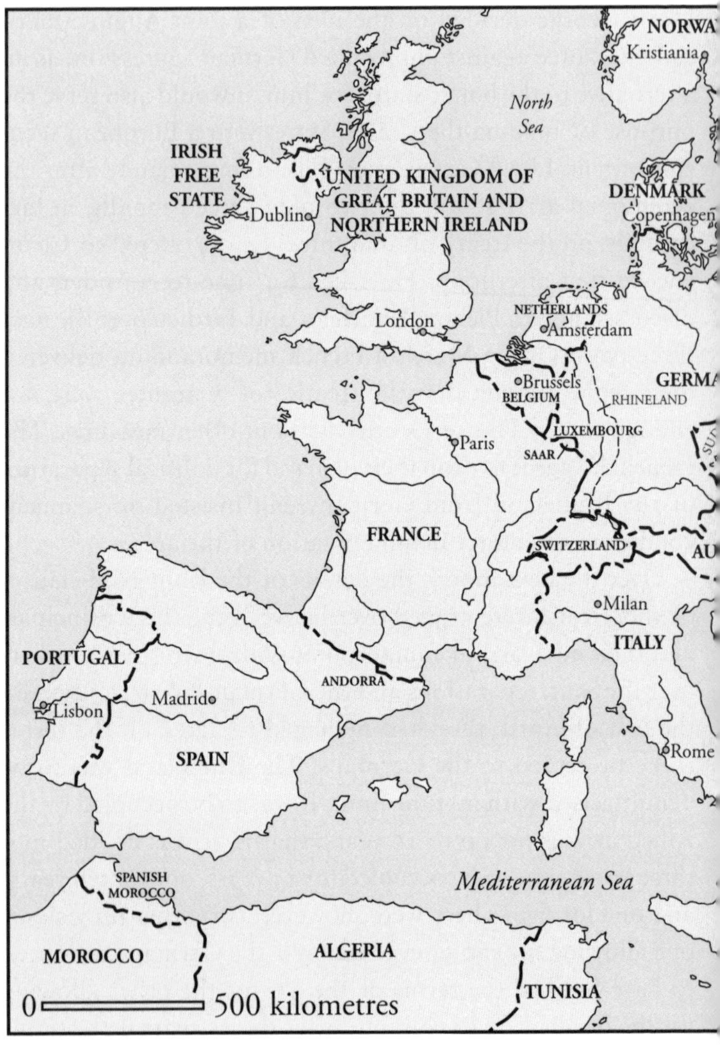
NORWA
Kristiania
North Sea
IRISH FREE STATE
Dublin
UNITED KINGDOM OF GREAT BRITAIN AND NORTHERN IRELAND
DENMARK
Copenhagen
London
NETHERLANDS
Amsterdam
Brussels
BELGIUM
GERMA
RHINELAND
LUXEMBOURG
Paris
SAAR
FRANCE
SWITZERLAND
AU
Milan
ITALY
PORTUGAL
ANDORRA
Lisbon
Madrid
SPAIN
Rome
SPANISH MOROCCO
Mediterranean Sea
MOROCCO
ALGERIA
TUNISIA
0 500 kilometres

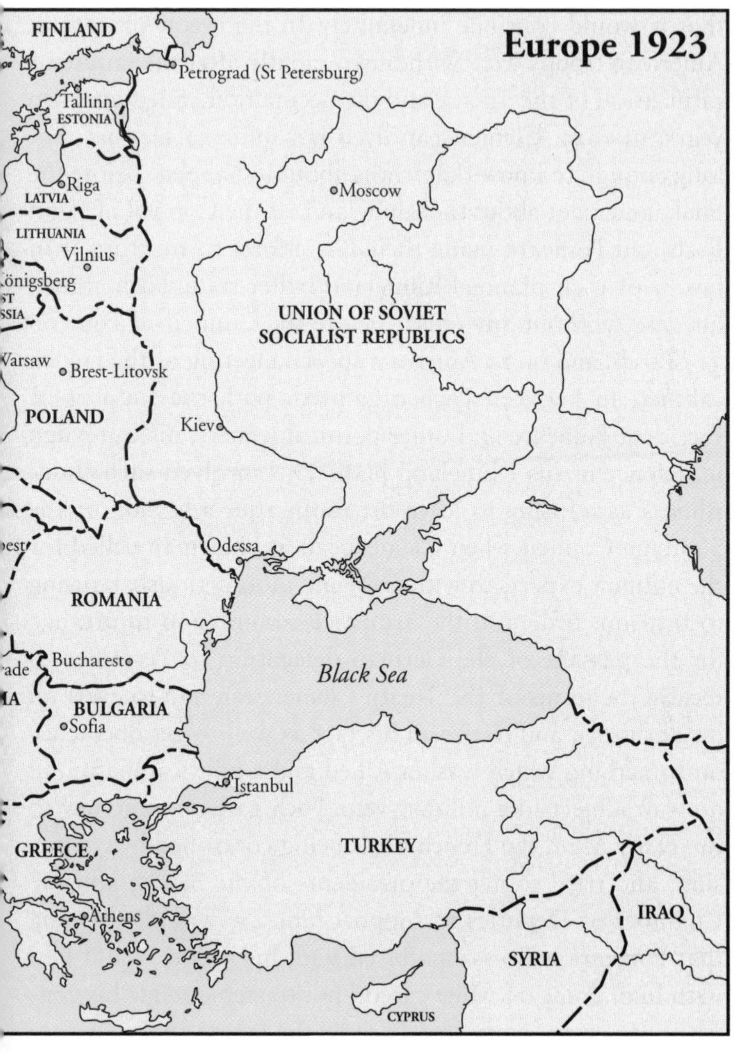
Europe 1923
FINLAND
Petrograd (St Petersburg)
Tallinn
ESTONIA
Riga
LATVIA
LITHUANIA
Vilnius
Moscow
UNION OF SOVIET
SOCIALIST REPUBLICS
Brest-Litovsk
POLAND
Kiev
Odessa
ROMANIA
Bucharest
BULGARIA
Sofia
Black Sea
Istanbul
TURKEY
GREECE
Athens
IRAQ
SYRIA
CYPRUS

that it would continue indefinitely. In the event, of course, American troops were withdrawn rapidly after the failure of ratification of the Treaty, and the occupation ended after ten years, in 1929. Clemenceau lived not quite to see that, but long enough to know that it was about to happen. Before the final agreement about the Rhineland, at the Council of Four, Foch and Poincaré made their last efforts to overturn it in favour of their planned Rhineland buffer state. Foch argued his case, without any effect, before the Council of Four on 31 March, and on 25 April at a special meeting of the French cabinet. In between Foch organised, with the support of President Poincaré and other political leaders, his campaign in defence of his Rhineland plan. This involved such childishness as refusing to leave the room after a session of the Supreme Council when Clemenceau as chairman called for the military experts to withdraw, and more seriously refusing to transmit orders to the armistice commission to arrange for the passage of the German delegation to Versailles to receive the terms of the Treaty. Clemenceau had to exert all his authority, and to use all his tact as well to get obedience on something which was an Allied and a political matter, in no way subject to a military veto. Foch gave an interview to the *Daily Mail*, the French press being controlled by censorship, and tried to get the presidents of the Senate and the Chamber of Deputies to support him. He was also hoping that Poincaré, who sympathised with his views, would join with him. Poincaré while careful not to step outside his constitutional role, supported Foch to the extent that he wrote to the prime minister insisting on a special cabinet meeting to hear Foch's objections with time to take account of them before the terms were presented to the German delegation. In a letter to Pichon of 19 April Poincaré gave his own view that a 15-year occupation was not enough of a guarantee, and that it must be reopened with the Allies. After a meeting with Clemenceau on 22 April, in which he pointed out the danger that the American Senate would not ratify the treaty of guarantee, Poincaré drafted a note expressing his view that the military occupation of the Rhineland had to continue for more than 15 years, until reparations had been fully paid. Finally on 25 April the special cabinet meeting to hear Foch was held, and proved to be a damp squib, as Poincaré himself said nothing.[4] The cabinet unanimously approved the terms that Clemenceau had achieved, and agreed that they should be submitted to the German delegation. Both Lloyd George and Woodrow Wilson, in defending the guarantee treaties to sceptical compatriots, stressed that they hardly amounted to anything more than the security promised to all members of the League of Nations, and hinted that they were only granted to give Clemenceau something with which to defeat his militarist and reactionary critics. This was not a promising start for Clemenceau's hope that he had in fact won something solid, amounting to a continuation of the wartime coalition against Germany.

The final question to be considered is that of the German-Polish frontier: it will not be examined in detail, which is matter for another volume, but simply as it related to the arguments between Wilson, Lloyd George and Clemenceau about the overall pattern of the Treaty. Polish affairs were important in this, as can be seen from one of the first confrontations in the Council of Four, on 27 March 1919. At that meeting Clemenceau responded to Lloyd George's Fontainebleau memorandum calling for moderate peace terms that would be acceptable to German opinion. Among other things, Clemenceau seized on Lloyd George's ideas about the German-Polish frontier. One of the difficulties was that Poland had been the topic of the 13th of Wilson's Fourteen Points, in typically vague and self-contradictory fashion. It stated; 'An independent Polish State should be erected which should include the territories inhabited by indisputably Polish populations, which should be assured a free and secure access to the sea … '

This formulation ignored the fact that in several crucial areas the German and Polish populations were intermingled, in some areas as the result of 40 years of deliberate German colonisation: it also ignored the fact that Poland's access to the sea inevitably went through areas with a German majority and the only port was the German city of Danzig: if Poland gained access to the sea by this route, the Germans of East Prussia would be separated from their compatriots by what became known as the Polish corridor. Only major ethnic cleansing, as happened in 1945, could overcome these problems, something inconceivable in 1919.

The Polish politician Roman Dmowski presented the Polish claims, which were extremely ambitious, to the Council of Ten on 29 January, but their progress through the system was slow. Although none of the major powers seriously considered the full Polish claim to re-establish the frontiers of Poland in 1772, which would have included millions of non-Poles, especially in the east, the French were much closer to the Polish position then either the British or Americans. However British and American experts on the relevant committees at first seemed to be ready to countenance much of the Polish programme. This indulgence was not to continue when Wilson and Lloyd George got involved, and Polish questions were discussed in the Council of Four on 27 March and afterwards. Lloyd George, in particular, expressed extremely negative views about the Poles. They seem to have been derived from the South African statesman J C Smuts who played a surprisingly influential role; perhaps also the junior advisor, L B Namier, himself a Jew from Galicia, played a part in Lloyd George's remarkably hostile view of Poland's claims. Clemenceau was far more sympathetic to Poland and at first supported the idea of giving it access to the Baltic Sea through Danzig in full sovereignty. However he fairly soon accepted the compromise solution of making Danzig a free city under the League of Nations. He also abandoned his support for including the Marienwerder district in the Polish corridor without a plebiscite of its overwhelming German majority. At this stage, and with very little discussion among the Council of Four, the other parts of the German-Polish frontier in Silesia were settled in a way favourable to Polish aspirations. It was in this area that the biggest concessions were made by the Allies in response to the German criticism of the draft terms. As a result, after a plebiscite in 1921, large areas of Silesia were retained by Germany. This retraction will be dealt with in Chapter 8; it can, however, be pointed out here that Clemenceau gave way far more readily on the Polish clauses than on those that directly concerned France.[5]

7

Reparations

Clemenceau himself took little part in negotiation of the reparations section of the Treaty, notwithstanding the fact that they were seen as an essential part of the settlement, vital for France's future. Economic and financial matters were never of much interest to him, and he left everything except the broadest of principles to others. As far as those broad principles were concerned, as has been already explained he was prepared to give ground on reparations in return for concessions from his allies on territorial matters. In any case it was on the territorial questions that he had to fight against Lloyd George and Wilson. On reparations he could let the British make the running, against American resistance. Contrary to what has often been stated in Anglo-Saxon accounts, it was not France but Britain that escalated the sums demanded in reparations into the stratosphere. Of course the British demands were only possible because of the strained interpretation of the term 'reparations' that developed when it was agreed that the costs of war pensions to widows and dependants could be included in the bill. If reparations had been limited to its original meaning, the costs of restoring damage to civilian property through German military action, the overwhelming majority would have been due to France and Belgium, with only a minimal amount for Britain. However, this was never an issue. Without doubt, the French calculation was that it was better for Britain to have an interest in achieving compensation from Germany, rather than hoping for British support for demands that would benefit only its allies.

Any discussion of the reparations section of the Treaty of Versailles demands as a preliminary the exposition of two basic points which have been succinctly and forcefully expressed by Sally Marks: 'The war had been fought on the soil of the victors: they were devastated and Germany was not. Most European belligerents had large domestic war debts: the victors had vast foreign ones as well, but Germany did not ... If the Allies, and especially France, had to assume reconstruction costs on top of domestic and foreign war debts, whereas Germany was left with only domestic debts, in the event eradicated by inflation, they would be the losers and German economic dominance would be tantamount to victory.'[1] These two points need to be stressed and elaborated. German territory had been almost untouched from the beginning to the end of the war, and its economic base emerged in 1918 stronger than it had ever been. Of course neither had Britain been invaded, but the position of France and Belgium was very different. Almost the whole of Belgium and that part of north-eastern France where much of its industry had been situated in 1914, had been in German hands for nearly all the war. It was not so much that the fighting itself had destroyed French and Belgian industry, although there was some of that: far more destruction was the result of deliberate German action in the last weeks of the war, as they retreated before the advancing Allied armies. It was then that the coalmines had been flooded, factories and farms had been laid waste, orchards cut down and livestock slaughtered or driven off to Germany. Previously it had been in the German interest to exploit the economy of the captured territories, and they had done so. The havoc wreaked in the autumn of 1918 was not unfortunate collateral damage, but deliberate destruction of a hated enemy's economic lifeblood. Thus it was hardly surprising that the Allies sought to impose the costs of reconstruction on Germany.

The second point was even more important for the future economic balance between victors and vanquished. Germany had negligible foreign debt. The Allies had vast debts, between themselves, and above all, to the United States. The essence of a complicated pattern was that Russia owed immense sums to both France and Britain, which few expected ever to be paid: Italy owed smaller amounts to Britain and France. France herself owed enormous sums to Britain and to the United States, while Britain, although a creditor *vis-à-vis* its allies, was enormously in debt to the United States. What really mattered was the triangular relationship involving Britain, France and the United States. At first the Europeans, France more optimistically than Britain, hoped that memory of wartime solidarity would produce at least some relaxation of the American demand for repayment to the last ounce of flesh. But they were rapidly disillusioned. Long before President Coolidge said 'They hired the money, didn't they', it was made clear to Britain and France that their war debts had to be repaid, in full, with interest. In these circumstances they were determined that Germany, without any war debts of its own, would be faced with an equal burden: otherwise, as in the case of the physical damage, Germany would be in a far better economic position than the victors.

Thus, although the war debt question was not itself on the agenda, and was not discussed in any way in the negotiation of the Treaty, it overshadowed the reparations negotiations like the ghost in Hamlet.

Another part of the background to the negotiations on reparations was the collapse of French aspirations for a new economic model for the post-war world, which would, they hoped, never return to the liberal system of 1914, in which only tariff protection, itself restricted by the ubiquity of most favoured nation clauses, limited free movement of goods, labour and capital. This model was influenced by ideas about German pre-war plans for economic domination, and by still more exaggerated suspicions of German post-war aspirations expressed in Friedrich Naumann's campaign for *Mittel Europa* (Central Europe) and other schemes for domination of Bolshevik Russia. The Allied economic conference at Paris in June 1916 was the high point of acceptance of such plans. The future envisaged seemed to be one in which the war had been ended without outright victory for either side, to be followed by a long-lasting armed truce between the rival coalitions, with the neutral United States on the margins. The scenario was one in which the Allies would continue to control the seas, and thus monopolise the major part of the economic resources of the world. This would allow them to hold back what they saw as the bid for economic domination that had emanated from Germany before and after 1914. While it is doubtful whether this ever had the support in British governmental circles that the French thought it had, British enthusiasm waned rapidly with the Russian collapse and the American arrival on the scene. The French government, however, continued to plan for post-war along these lines. Etienne Clémentel, who was Minister of Commerce and

Industry from 1916 to November 1919, was an enthusiast. He developed a special section in his ministry, headed by the economic historian, Henri Hauser, which elaborated plans for the post-war world, both domestic and international in scope. Hauser, who was a historian of the Mercantilist period of the 15th to 18th centuries, saw 19th-century liberalism as a temporary Anglo-Saxon aberration from which the world could now be rescued. Such illusions were strongly encouraged in the last 12 months of the war when American participation led to the development of inter-Allied economic and financial co-operation on a huge scale, developing out of shipping control and the convoy system made necessary by the economic blockade of Germany and U-boat warfare. Clémentel and other French governmental figures were slow to realise that the Americans would want a return to the free market as soon as the war ended, and that, after a little hesitation, the British would follow suit. Debates in the Supreme Economic Council from January to April 1919 revealed the fundamental divergence between the French and the Anglo-Saxons on these matters. Clémentel later wrote a substantial book on wartime Allied co-operation and its demise. He ended it with the meeting of the Raw Materials section of the Supreme Economic Council on 4 April 1919, which, he said, marked the end of Allied economic solidarity. He concludes sadly: 'because of this error, the peace was incomplete: it lacked that spirit of altruism and of disinterested co-operation among allies that had so powerfully contributed to victory.'[2]

Wartime co-operation had also included financial solidarity; in practice this meant British support for the French franc. The British authorities believed with justification that their taxpayers had accepted an enormous burden in order to avoid or at least reduce, the inflationary results of the war. Their allies had financed their war efforts by creating money in disguised ways. Financial solidarity among allies would simply mean France getting a free ride at the expense of Britain for the indefinite future. Soon after the armistice the British government took steps to halt this, warning French financial experts who came to London in November 1918. The first attempt to end support for the franc was made on 3 January 1919, but was postponed in the face of hysterical protests. In his memoirs, the French finance minister Klotz blamed Keynes for the change of British policy. He wrote that Keynes had pro-German and pro-Bolshevik views, and was very anti-French, and that his influence became predominant when Bonar Law was replaced as Chancellor of the Exchequer by Austen Chamberlain. According to Klotz, Keynes was thus responsible for all the currency instability that afflicted the post-war world: 'This monetary megalomania is the true cause of the financial catastrophe which has befallen the Universe.' In fact there was no chance that Britain would continue to support the French franc, or other Allied currencies, without backing from the United States, which was certainly not forthcoming. After the same meeting in Paris on 19 February that inspired Klotz' outburst, Austen Chamberlain wrote to his sister: 'The financial problems which assail me grow more and more difficult. The French are very chauvinistic and will not cut their coat according to their cloth. They think they should clothe themselves at my expense … Both France and Italy are in queer street … and if I am not careful I shall find that they have dragged me into it before long. And meanwhile … America is now as much all out for business as for a few short months she was all out for war. The president with his lofty ideals and all his high faluting is surrounded by what Keynes calls "a lot of Wall Street toughs", and tough enough they are.' After further protests the French franc was finally abandoned to its fate in March 1919, beginning a slow slide that led to its stabilisation in 1926 at one fifth of its 1914 value relative to the pound sterling.[3]

The Reparations Commission was appointed on 25 January 1919, the French delegates being the finance minister, Louis Lucien Klotz, Louis Loucheur, and the young Albert Lebrun. Like the other commissions that laboured through the first two months of 1919, it failed to resolve the problems it faced, which had then to be passed to the 'Big Four' in their face to face discussions in late March and April. In fact they also failed to resolve crucial points, which were left to the post-treaty Reparations Commission which only finalised matters (in theory) with the London Schedule of Payments in May 1921.

'The French are very chauvinistic and will not cut their coat according to their cloth. They think they should clothe themselves at my expense ... Both France and Italy are in queer street ... and if I am not careful I shall find that they have dragged me into it before long.'
AUSTEN CHAMBERLAIN

The reparations question was that part of the settlement where the fact that the armistice had emerged from a German appeal to President Wilson alone introduced the most equivocation. He had declared in one of his supplementary pronouncements (the Four Ends speech of 11 February 1918) that there should be no punitive indemnities. Aware of the limitation this would place on their financial demands, Britain and France had insisted on the insertion in the armistice of a clause stating that Germany agreed to compensate the victors for all damage done to the civilian population of the Allies and their property by the aggression of Germany, by land, by sea and from the air. Thus there should not have been any question of demanding the full cost of the war from Germany, but British and French public opinion had been led to believe that Germany would be made to pay the full cost of the war. This was blatantly true of Britain where it figured in the November election campaign, and was endorsed in so many words by government ministers. There was no election campaign in France, and the position is less clear-cut. Klotz was supposed to have declared that 'Germany will pay', with the implication that he meant it would pay the full cost of the war. In fact it would be more likely that he referred to reconstruction of the devastated areas, and in any case, proof of his saying it has never been produced. Nevertheless the Commission on Reparation of Damage was at once presented with demands for the full cost of the war by all its members except the Americans. However, these claims were rejected by the American members.

In any case it was obvious that a bill for the entire cost of the war would be astronomical and impossible. In fact the political leaders were already saying to each other, although not to their publics, that even reconstruction of the damaged areas of France and Belgium would be beyond Germany's capacity for payment. Thus, although the full extent of German liability was discussed at length, it was always with the proviso that capacity to pay, how much and over what period, was equally important. These questions were discussed by the Reparations Commission in January and February 1919. In the course of these discussions, and as a compromise move, the young American John Foster Dulles, later famous as the hawkish Secretary of State in the 1950s, suggested what became Article 231 of the Treaty, the War Guilt Clause. This stated that 'Germany accepts the responsibility of Germany and its allies for causing all the damage to which the Allied and Associated Governments and their nationals have been subjected as a consequence of the war imposed on them by the aggression of Germany and her allies.' It was immediately followed by Article 232 stating that 'the resources of Germany are not adequate to make complete reparation for all such loss and damage' and continuing to demand 'compensation for all damage done to the civilian population'. Far from being intended to humiliate the enemy, Dulles saw these two articles as a way of differentiating between the moral entitlement of the Allies and their actual demands. The way it would be seen by the Germans was not foreseen. When these two clauses were discussed by the leaders, Clemenceau closed discussion, saying, *it is simply a matter of drafting*. It was the public response of the German delegation that turned these clauses into one of the chief elements in the whole German diatribe against the Treaty. They had not been introduced by the French as a red rag to the German bull, but by the young American as an ingenious piece of drafting.[4]

It is simply a matter of drafting.
CLEMENCEAU

The Reparations Commission continued its discussions of the related questions of German liabilities and its capacity to pay, and of the distribution of the proceeds. There was also the question of whether Germany would or would not be presented with a fixed sum as the total of its liability. All of these questions impacted on each other. If the Allies agreed on a total, and on the distribution among themselves, it did not matter much how the total was arrived at. But on the other hand, if there was no fixed sum, and liability was calculated by adding up different claims under different headings, the definition of what were legitimate claims was vital. In practice this meant the question of whether the money paid by the Allies as pensions to veterans and their dependants be included as damage to civilians and their property. If pensions were not included, the great majority of the payments would go to France and Belgium, as Britain and the British Empire had suffered little physical damage except for shipping losses. In spite of this France agreed from the first to the inclusion of pensions, and added their own pension costs to those of reconstruction of the devastated areas.

French critics have taken Clemenceau to task for this, but he probably felt that it was better to give Britain a stake of its own in reparations, rather than expecting it to fight for reparations that would go overwhelmingly to France and Belgium. The French delegation did argue at first for priority to be given to reparation of physical damage, but then abandoned this position. The argument between the Allies was then simply about the share that each would get. On 26 March 1919 Loucheur asked for a French/British share of 72:18, with the remainder for Belgium. In fact no agreement could be reached before the signature of the Treaty, and Britain and France eventually agreed on 52:22 at Spa in June 1920. In the meantime they presented a joint front against American reluctance to include pensions in the reparations demands. Finally the South African delegate Jan Christian Smuts was able to get Wilson to agree. On 1 April Wilson declared: 'Logic! Logic! I don't give a damn for logic. I am going to include pensions.' In any case it would not affect the total sum demanded, but only its distribution among the Allies.[5]

Thus when reparations, along with all the other important questions, came before the Council of Four in late March and April 1919, the main question was German capacity to pay.

Significantly the British appeal for moderation in the Fontainebleau memorandum was extremely vague about reparations. In practice it was Britain and France that were now arguing for very large sums, and also for not naming any total sum in the Treaty itself. On 5 April the Council of Four agreed that Germany would make a preliminary payment of £1,000 million in gold by May 1921. Against French opposition it was decided that this sum would go first towards the costs of the army of occupation, and for imports of food and raw materials. Only if there were anything left over would it be for reparations. It was agreed on 12 April not to fix any total sum in the Treaty itself. This was to be decided by May 1921 by a Reparations Commission consisting of one representative each for the United States, France, Britain and Italy, with the fifth place alternating between Belgium, Japan and Yugoslavia. Other matters left for the Commission were how and when Germany should pay, and what rate of interest should be charged. Payments were, in principle, to be completed within 30 years, but with provision for postponement. All major decisions had to be unanimous, thus giving each government a veto. There was further discussion about measures to be taken if the Germans defaulted on payments. France wanted strict penalties, but Britain and the United States resisted. The Council of Four on 25 April approved an extremely vague clause drafted by Wilson, which the Anglo-Saxons thought limited any sanctions to economic and financial measures but which did not specifically say so. A clause allowing 'such other measures as the respective governments may determine to be necessary', was used by the French to justify the occupation of the Ruhr in 1923.[6]

Working out the details of the reparations clauses of the Treaty, which as much as anything involved disguised reductions in the sums demanded, took place long after Clemenceau left office and will not be discussed here. But an overall assessment of reparations, and Clemenceau's role in that part of the Treaty is required, above all because of the central part played by reparations in the negative verdict on the peace settlement arrived at by so many.

Thus a brief recapitulation is called for, to point out in the first place that the often-stated view that paying reparations damaged the German economy, and thus undermined the social and political stability of the Weimar Republic cannot be correct. What seems to be meant is the hyperinflation of 1922–3, and the subsequent and equally devastating deflation of 1929–31. But the inflation, contrary to contemporary German claims cannot have been caused by reparations payments, as only negligible sums had been paid up to that time. The inflation's roots went back to wartime financial irresponsibility, based on the hope that after a German victory its defeated enemies would pay; the irresponsibility was continued by the social welfare policies of post-war governments. Certainly a big factor in the failure of German governments between 1919 and 1923 to even try to prevent hyperinflation was their desire to demonstrate that they could not make reparations payments. Only in this sense can reparations be seen as a cause of the destruction of the currency. Most recent analysis has reached the view that the payments actually demanded by the Allies in 1921–3, as opposed to the astronomical sums dangled before the British and French publics in 1919, could have been paid if the German governments of the time had so willed.[7] Of course they did not do so until brought to their senses by the complete collapse of the mark and consequential disruption to normal life as a result of the policy of passive resistance to the French occupation of the

Ruhr. The tragedy of all this was real enough even if it was caused not by reparations, but by the German refusal to pay reparations. Another aspect of this disaster is that Germany was allowed to drive a wedge between Britain and France. Having insisted at least as much as France on the reparations clauses of the Treaty, Britain refused in 1922 and 1923 to help France in its attempt to enforce payments. This sorry story illustrated everything Clemenceau had said in 1919 about the necessity of enforcing the Treaty on an unwilling Germany. If Lloyd George wanted a treaty that Germany would willingly accept, it would have had to have been one that was far less harsh; it would in fact have had to be a treaty not far removed from one suitable after German victory.

The Reparations Commission fixed the sum Germany should pay in May 1921 at 132,000 million gold marks, provoking the German response that it was far beyond their possibilities of payment. In response to Allied threats Germany made limited payments for six months before suspending them on the grounds that the fall in the value of the German currency made it impossible. This impasse eventually led in January 1923 to the occupation of the Ruhr by French and Belgian troops, in the face of British opposition. The occupation did force Germany eventually to return to the negotiating table, but it was the summer of 1924 before a solution was found in the form of the Dawes Plan. By that time the intransigent Poincaré had been replaced as French prime minister by the weak, conciliatory and incompetent Herriot.

It would be far beyond the scope of this study to follow the development of reparations over this and subsequent years. The main points to be emphasised are firstly that the German economy cannot have been destroyed by reparations that were hardly paid: insofar as payment was made between 1925 and

1931 it was financed by loans, mainly subscribed to in the United States, which were then defaulted on. Secondly that France was left without either British or American support in its attempts to enforce the reparations clauses between 1921 and 1924. This Allied disunity encouraged German attempts to break free from the constraints imposed by the Treaty. Another topic on which there was wide divergence between British and French views, but on which Clemenceau failed to press the French case was that of the limitation of German armaments. The British were left to draw up the naval clauses more or less as they wished, while the future German army was also limited according to British ideas. Foch and his military advisors advocated a small, short-service conscript army, with volunteer officers. But the British rejected conscription, and the German army was to be entirely a long-serving professional force. Clemenceau clearly thought that other questions were of more importance, and this issue was decided as early as 17 March. In fact the system adopted facilitated the rapid expansion of the German army after 1934 as it provided a nucleus of highly-trained men who could become officers and NCOs in the new mass conscript army.

8

German Signature and the Other Treaties

By the last week of April the Council of Four had made enough progress to envisage the final drafting of the terms to be presented to the German government. Accordingly it was asked to send a delegation, which arrived at Versailles on 30 April. It was headed by the Foreign Minister, Count Ulrich von Brockdorff-Rantzau. An aristocrat and former army officer turned diplomat, Brockdorff-Rantzau was above all a fierce German nationalist, who had transferred his loyalty to the Republic. He had shown his disregard for mere ideological details by being one of the organisers of Lenin's journey to Russia through Germany in 1917, a pro-Bolshevik stance, which he continued in his capacity as ambassador in Moscow in the 1920s. Above all he was imbued by hatred of France, and he appeared to be unable to recognise that Germany had been defeated. His arrogant reception of the terms completely alienated the Allied negotiators before he returned to Germany to advise his government not to sign.

The Allied note had made it clear that the Germans were to be presented with a treaty to which they could suggest changes only in writing, and there would be no Peace Congress of the nature of the 1815 Congress of Vienna. Nevertheless the German delegation brought a team of experts with them, and was indignant at this treatment, which they described as making the Treaty a 'Diktat'. In reality of course, the Allies did react to the German objections, and some major changes to the draft terms were made before the final signature. If Lloyd George and the British delegation had had their way the changes would have been greater still, but as President Wilson in general supported Clemenceau in resisting what they saw as weakness in the face of German arrogance, the greater part of the terms that had been so painfully hammered out by April were retained.

Driven on by Tardieu, the experts and officials managed to produce the text of the Treaty that was printed and ready to be presented to the German delegation on 7 May. A plenary session of the Allied and Associated Powers was held on 6 May and was presented with a summary of the draft terms. Foch once again recorded his protest at their failure to deprive Germany of its sovereignty over the left bank of the Rhine. For the first time the press presented the terms of peace to the general public. In France there was an outburst of disappointment as the terms were revealed. It was on 8 May 1919 that Jacques Bainville,

ACTION FRANÇAISE

The Ligue d'Action Française was a movement of the extreme Right emerging out of the nationalist activity of the anti-Dreyfusards between 1899 and 1906. Its leading theorist, Charles Maurras (1868–1952), developed an ideology of integral nationalism, monarchism, and Catholicism, that is a programme for the rejection of the Republic and of the French Revolution. It had negligible success in Parliamentary politics, but great influence as a literary and intellectual movement. Its newspaper, also *l'Action Française*, published daily from 1908 to 1944, was at the peak of its prestige at the end of the war. Jacques Bainville was seen as a major historian and political commentator.

in an article in the newspaper *L'Action Française,* coined his famous phrase 'Une paix trop douce pour ce qu'elle a de dur' (a peace too weak for its severity), a judgement which he later developed into his book *Les Conséquences Politiques de la Paix*, published in 1920.

On 7 May the formal presentation of the Treaty to the German plenipotentiaries took place in the Hôtel Trianon at Versailles, where, as Lloyd George recalled in his Memoirs, the Supreme War Council had met less than a year before to the sound of the German heavy artillery thudding in the distance. As President, Clemenceau made the only speech on behalf of the Allies. It was brief and informed the German delegation that there would be no oral discussion of the terms, although they could make written responses within 15 days, a time limit later extended.

Such was the stridency of Count Brockdorff-Rantzau's speech that it antagonised his audience and was to result in Wilson and Clemenceau's entrenched resistance to Lloyd George's attempts to weaken the Treaty's terms. He maintained that Germany would not take sole responsibility for war crimes, but it was prepared to join with its former enemies 'in showing mankind new goals of political and social progress' on the basis of a programme drawn up by impartial experts. Only in that way could Germany fulfil its obligation to restore Northern France and Belgium. To impose impossible financial burdens on Germany would make this reparation impossible and destroy the whole European economic system. The only way of preventing this collapse would be 'the economic and social solidarity of all nations in a free and all-comprising League of Nations. The German people will resign themselves to their hard lot, if the bases of the peace, as initially agreed upon, are not destroyed. A peace which cannot be defended before the world as a peace of justice would always evoke new resistance. No one could sign it with a clear conscience, for it could not be carried out.'[1]

On 9 May Brockdorff-Rantzau sent a brief note rejecting the Treaty completely: 'the basis of the peace of justice mutually agreed upon has been abandoned ... The draft treaty includes demands which are intolerable for any nation. In the opinion of our experts, many of these demands cannot be met. The German delegation will make good this contention point by point.'[2]

Clemenceau replied that there was no question of changing the whole structure of the Treaty, and that only practical suggestions about particular points could be considered. This led to a series of exchanges on minor points, but little of substance. Meanwhile the Council of Four got on with preparing the treaties for Austria and Hungary. As the expiry of the time limit drew near the German delegation asked for a seven-day extension, which was granted. The leading members of the delegation then travelled to Spa to discuss matters with members of the German government, returning with their authority to make the best terms they could with the Allies. By 29 May Brockdorff-Rantzau had produced a reply consisting of general criticism of the Treaty as a whole, and of detailed counter-proposals on specific points.

In the course of discussing many other topics by the Council of Four, in reply to a question from Lloyd George, Clemenceau stated on 28 May that he thought that Germany would sign the Treaty but with the firm intention of not executing it. His unofficial representative in Berlin, Professor Haguenin had learned from Philipp Scheidemann, the German Chancellor, that after signing the Treaty the government would resign and would be replaced by the Independent Socialists.

The ensuing chaos would force the Allies to occupy Germany and administer it themselves. This produced no further discussion amongst the Council of Four. The next day, 29 May, President Wilson raised the question of the Allied military occupation of the Rhineland. Lloyd George took this up, and pointed out that as the costs of the occupation were to be imposed on Germany with priority over reparations, they would reduce what could be paid under the latter category. In any case he thought that the idea of a 15-year occupation had been accepted too easily and should be reconsidered. Clemenceau replied that he certainly agreed with Wilson that the occupation was a political and not a purely military question, but that he could not accept that a question that they had decided between them should now be reopened. To which Lloyd George responded with an enigmatic threat: 'England, being one of the powers that has contributed to victory, has the right to share in the final decision.' President Wilson then said the United States could only contribute a token contingent to the occupying force. Finally they decided to appoint a committee to study the details of the occupation.[3]

On 2 June Lloyd George returned to the attack, making a determined attempt to modify the terms in response to the German objections. This followed meetings of the British delegation, and of special meetings in Paris of members of the cabinet and the Imperial War Cabinet. These meetings, on 31 May and on 1 and 2 June, saw Churchill and Smuts pressing particularly hard for concessions. The American delegation also met on 3 June, for the first and only time meeting as a whole with all its experts and the President himself. The American experts had much the same reaction as the British; as Professor Shotwell put it: 'when all the [German] sacrifices were added together, the whole was greater than the sum of the parts.' But the President did not respond to his advisors as did Lloyd George; he took virtually no part in the confrontation between Lloyd George and Clemenceau on 2 June.[4]

Lloyd George began with the threat that Britain would refuse to resume hostilities, or even reimpose the blockade if the Germans refused to sign the Treaty, when the terms had been modified. All strands of opinion in Britain and the Empire supported this view. The following points had been put to him, as areas where changes had to be made: the German-Polish frontier, the Saar, reparations and the military occupation of the Rhineland. However, he had convinced his colleagues that the Saar should be left as it was. Clemenceau replied that this revealed a most serious situation. He also had to deal with his public opinion, which felt that he had already made too any concessions. *We all want to finish as soon as possible: You think that the way is to make concessions, we think it is to press on (brusquer). We know the Germans better than you: the more concessions we make, the more they will demand.* Nevertheless, he was prepared to consider some modifications. The details of the German-Polish frontier were not intangible, but it should be remembered that a strong Poland was needed as a barrier between Germany and Russia. Similarly there could be changes in detail about reparations and the military occupation, but the basic principles must be upheld.

'To his horror Mr Lloyd George, desiring at the last moment all the moderation he dared, discovered that he could not in five days persuade the President of error in what it had taken five months to prove to him to be just and right. After all it was harder to de-bamboozle this old Presbyterian than it had been to bamboozle him.'

JOHN MAYNARD KEYNES[5]

The occupation was not needed to prevent a German attack on France. It was because Germany would sign the Treaty with the intention of not carrying it out. If the Allies had no means of putting pressure on it to execute the terms, everything would leak away. He ended with an emotional appeal to Allied unity: *My policy at the Conference has been one of a close understanding with Britain and America. I know that you have great interests far away. I know something of the American continent, and of the immense achievements of the British Empire. Because I have made understanding with England and America the basis of my policy, I am attacked from all sides as weak and incompetent. If I were to disappear you would find yourself in the presence of even bigger divergences … I refuse to believe that we must suspend our negotiations because we cannot give a common answer to the Germans.* Lloyd George returned to the question of the occupation, saying that his colleagues had told him that he should never have agreed to it, and that the British cabinet was unanimous that he should have given France the alternative of the occupation or a treaty of guarantee and not both. Clemenceau replied: *I have the duty to be frank. I say now, with full knowledge of the significance of my words, that I can make no concession on this point: it is impossible.* Wilson asked if he could concede something on the costs of the occupation. Clemenceau replied, yes, as long as the principle was maintained. Otherwise he would resign and the President of the Republic would have to find someone to negotiate on this new basis. The session ended with them appointing a committee to look again at reparations.[6]

The Council of Four continued their acrimonious discussion over the next few days. In the end the biggest changes to the terms first offered to the Germans were in relation to the

German-Polish frontier. As a result of plebiscites, not originally envisaged, Marienwerder and Allenstein voted to remain in Germany, while Upper Silesia was eventually divided between Germany and Poland. In spite of talking about the need for changing the reparations clauses, Lloyd George failed to push this matter through, while on the Allied occupation of the Rhineland he was met with Clemenceau's absolute refusal to go back on what had been agreed. Wilson did not support Lloyd George on this, although he had already indicated that the American army would have only a token representation in the Allied force. As Lloyd George dropped the Saar question and the Polish frontier, and reparations were passed to sub-committees, the Council of Four (apart from discussing other topics such as the Austrian treaty), mainly concerned itself with the British reservations about the military occupation. On 13 June, two other members of the British cabinet, the Conservative Bonar Law, and Labour's George Barnes, were heard in support of Lloyd George's arguments. Finally, as his ultimate concession, Clemenceau was persuaded to agree to a clause allowing the reduction of the period of occupation to less than 15 years, if Germany had given proof of its intention to fulfil all the obligations it had assumed by signing the Treaty. But he refused to fix any date for that, so that he could say to his own public that the occupation would continue indefinitely if Germany had not fulfilled its obligations.[7] Even this did not end Lloyd George's attempts to renege on his agreement to the occupation. On 25 June, only three days before the final signature of the Treaty, Mordacq wrote that Lloyd George suddenly appeared at Clemenceau's office in the Ministry of War to say that Britain could not agree to the occupation of the Rhineland. Mordacq stated that Clemenceau at once went to see President Wilson who told Lloyd

George that he must respect the promises he had made, and that if Lloyd George refused to sign the Treaty, he would at once leave for the United States, explaining his reasons to the whole world.[8]

These modified terms were drafted and presented to the German delegation on 16 June. Meanwhile the Council of Four had called in Marshal Foch and General Weygand to advise on the steps to be taken if the German government refused to sign. Much to Clemenceau's annoyance the two military men tried to take this last opportunity to influence political matters. Clemenceau wanted a rapid march on Berlin if the German government refused to sign the Treaty: any hesitation, he thought, would give the impression that demobilisation had already sapped Allied military superiority. But whereas on 10 and 19 May Foch had stated that there would be no problem about an advance on Berlin, he now made difficulties, and declared that he did not have enough troops for a direct march on Berlin. Instead he proposed a slow advance through the south German states, with separate armistices or even peace treaties arranged separately with Baden, Württemberg, Bavaria, and so on. It was the resurrection of his plan for breaking up Germany into separate states that had been turned down by all the political leaders, including his own. Clemenceau thought that Weygand had put him up to this manoeuvre. The generals were sent away to produce their plans in writing, which they did the next day, 17 June. Finally on 20 June there was a meeting of the Supreme War Council, at which Clemenceau, Wilson, Balfour, and Sonnino were joined by all the military leadership, including General Robertson and Sir Henry Wilson for Britain, and Foch, Pétain and Weygand for France. Foch again presented his plan for an advance by stages along the Maine valley in southern

Germany, with the conclusion of successive armistices with the different German states. Clemenceau pointed out that this would involve a complete recasting of the Treaty. But matters were to some extent left in the air, presumably as the politicians believed that in any case the German government would sign, so that the whole matter was hypothetical.[9]

Having received the Allied reply, Brockdorff-Rantzau and most important figures in the German delegation returned to consult with their government, recommending a refusal. The Allies had demanded a reply in three days, extended to five, and then to seven. On 20 June Brockdorff-Rantzau resigned as foreign minister, which entailed the collapse of the Scheidemann government. The new cabinet, headed by the Socialist Gustav Bauer, decided that they had no alternative but to accept the Treaty. But they still hoped to get Articles 227–230 deleted, the ones that demanded the trial of the Kaiser and other war criminals. When the Allies refused to accept these qualifications, at 5.30 p.m. on 24 June, one and a half hours before the deadline, Germany accepted the Treaty. Soon afterwards news reached Paris that the German fleet, interned at Scapa Flow, had been scuttled by its German officers and crew. As this was, of course, a blatant violation of the terms of the armistice, it gave indication of the difficulties the Allies would face in enforcing the treaty on a recalcitrant Germany. On 28 June, the two new German plenipotentiaries were received in the Hall of Mirrors in the Palace of Versailles for the brief ceremony of the formal signing of the Treaty. This place had been chosen because on 18 January 1871 it had been chosen by the victors of the Franco-Prussian War for the proclamation of the second German Empire.

Clemenceau's role in the other parts of the peace settlement must now be considered. In fact only the treaties of

St Germain with Austria, and Neuilly with Bulgaria, were concluded before he left office in January 1920, but the main lines of the Treaty of Trianon with Hungary, signed only on 4 June 1920 had been already decided. The question of making peace with the Ottoman Empire is more complicated. Clemenceau's role here is of some importance, and the quarrel between France and Britain about their respective shares in the spoils began soon after the armistice. But the settlement here remained undecided until long after he left office. Not only was the Treaty of Sèvres not concluded until 10 August 1920, but it proved to be completely inoperable because of the Turkish national revival under Kemal Ataturk, with whom another treaty was concluded at Lausanne in 1923. This means that Clemenceau's departure left everything in this area ongoing, part of a long and complicated story, which will be dealt with elsewhere. This section will deal only with the Franco-British conflict over the Middle East before Clemenceau resigned, and with the small part he played in the treaties with Austria, Bulgaria and Hungary. For the most part he did not think that that vital French interests were at stake in these treaties, and he played a far less central role than in the German treaty. That said, Clemenceau gave a good deal of his time in the summer and autumn of 1919 to taking part in the meetings of what were now called the Heads of Delegations debating the other treaties after Wilson and Lloyd George had left Paris.

There were two major questions involved in the Treaty of St Germain with Austria. The first was the prohibition of a union between Austria and Germany, *Anschluss* as it was called: the second the decision to make the frontier between the new Czechoslovakia and Germany the pre-war frontier between Germany and Austria-Hungary. This meant that about two million Germans, the so-called Sudeten Germans, would be make citizens of Czechoslovakia. With hindsight based on the events of 1938–9 these two decisions seem crucial in the link between the peace settlement of 1919 and the outbreak of the Second World War. This is true whether the link is seen as in the eyes of the appeasers as being the crucial element by which the 1919 settlement betrayed Wilsonian principles, or whether it is seen as the failure to uphold the treaties of 1919 in the case of German determination to destroy them. And yet, in 1919 there was remarkably little debate about these matters.

Anschluss was put on the agenda in that it was demanded by both the new Austrian and German governments from very early on in their existence. Ebert and Brockdorff-Rantzau demanded it in the Weimar Assembly in February 1919: as the latter said: 'The German people is a living unity beyond all state boundaries, even beyond the old Empire.'[10] He went on to sign a protocol with the Austrian Dr Otto Bauer on 2 March preparing for the union of Germany and Austria. In fact there was no possibility that the Allies would allow this union, which would have created a more powerful Germany than that of 1914, and whose geography would have at once posed a threat to Czechoslovakia. Clemenceau had already told Colonel House that *Anschluss* could not be allowed. On 27 March, as part of his reply to Lloyd George's Fontainebleau memorandum he reiterated this prohibition. His statement was not contested by Lloyd George or by House deputising for the absent Wilson: nor did Wilson react later. Various American missions, and the French Allizé mission to Vienna, reported that Austrian public opinion was not unanimously in favour of union with Germany. Whether or not that was correct, it was simply not going to be allowed by the victors. In spite of all their protestations in favour of a moderate peace, acceptable to German opinion, neither Wilson nor Lloyd George raised the issue in a serious way.

There was more debate among the Allied delegations about the frontiers of Czechoslovakia, but still not very much. Eduard Beneš, Czech minister of foreign affairs, presented his case to the Council of Ten on 5 February 1919, emphasising and exaggerating the contribution of the Czech Legion to Allied victory. The Legion was, of course, still fighting in Russia, but by this time fighting against Bolshevism, not Germany. The Czech claim to the whole of the historic provinces of Bohemia and Moravia, including their German inhabitants, was then examined by a sub-committee, in which some arguments were presented about the danger of their resentment: on the other hand Czech aspirations to extend the old frontier at certain points were rejected. The question came before the Council of Four on 4 April, at the peak of the conflict over the Rhineland. Clemenceau simply declared in favour of maintaining the 1914 frontier. Lloyd George agreed without any argument, as did House for the United States. Neither then nor later did Wilson try to change this decision. Thus what were later seen as crucial elements in the overall settlement provoked very little discussion.[11]

Making peace with Hungary proved more difficult, and took much more of Clemenceau's time, although French vital interests were not at stake. The reason for the difficulty was the rule of the Bolshevik Bela Kun between 21 March and 4 August 1919, complicated by the difficulty of persuading Romania to withdraw its army from Budapest back to the frontier decided by the negotiators in Paris. Along with his colleagues in Paris Clemenceau must share the blame for allowing Hungary to be treated more harshly and unfairly than any of the defeated enemies except the Ottoman Empire. The Treaty of Trianon reduced Hungary to one-third of its former territory, and left one-third of the Magyar nation as minorities in its neighbour states. As a result, throughout the inter-war period Hungary was eager to overthrow the 1919 settlement if ever the possibility emerged. It must be admitted that Clemenceau simply allowed this to happen without being much concerned. In the summer of 1919 he wanted above all to avoid the use of French troops in the area; although the French contingent there was small, neither Britain nor the United States had any forces that could be deployed, and he was concerned that over-emphatic declarations on the victors' part might fall to the French to implement. Thus any idea of a crusade against Bolshevism in Hungary was vetoed, and the territorial settlement resulted from the invasions of Hungary conducted by its neighbours, Romania, Czechoslovakia and Yugoslavia. The statesmen in Paris did not have the military force to achieve boundary changes, even if they had wanted to. One of the most absurd of the charges levied against Clemenceau by his critics was that he had, out of spite resulting from the Count Czernin incident of March 1918, destroyed the Austro-Hungarian Empire.

On 2 April 1918, Count Czernin, the Austro-Hungarian Foreign Minister, issued a public statement announcing that France had approached him to ask for peace terms. Clemenceau's response was simple: *Count Czernin has lied.* As Clemenceau was able to prove this, and to show that in reality Austria-Hungary had approached France seeking peace terms, the result was Czernin's resignation. As Clemenceau explained to the Foreign Affairs Commission of the Senate on 8 May 1918, *I could not allow it to be thought that at the time*

I summed up my policy in the words 'I wage war', I was lying and that I was asking Count Czernin for peace.[12]

Whether he welcomed the collapse of Austria-Hungary, or deplored it, neither Clemenceau nor any of the Allied statesmen had the power to resist the movements of the former subject nationalities that swept away the empire in October 1918. Although the heads of delegations meeting in Paris spent a good deal of time discussing events in Hungary and south-eastern Europe, they had very little control over them. Keynes made the break-up of Europe, portrayed as being an economic unit before 1914, one of his charges against the peacemakers of 1919. But it is difficult to see how they could have hoped to preserve the economic unity even of the territory of the former Austria-Hungary: the idea of creating a Danubian economic federation was building castles in Spain.

The situation in the territories of the former Ottoman Empire provided another example where the self-imposed responsibilities of the statesmen in Paris vastly exceeded their power to control events. In this case it was the midsummer of 1920, long after Clemenceau had left office, before reality began to dawn. The Treaty of Sèvres itself was only drawn up between February and April 1920, after he had resigned and departed on holiday. There is therefore little point in discussing the details of the arrangements which were supposed to be imposed on Turkey, arrangements with which he had little to do, and which proved ephemeral when challenged by the nationalist revival led by Kemal. It can simply be noted that, casually and without debate, in a meeting of the Council of Four on 6 May 1919, he concurred in the landing of Greek troops at Smyrna (Izmir), the catalyst that led to the transformation of the Turkish situation. In response to Woodrow

Wilson's questions as to whether they had any objections to the Greek disembarkation, both Lloyd George and Clemenceau simply said that they had none. But 'this diplomatic decision, perhaps one of the least defensible of the 20th century', was primarily due to Lloyd George. Clemenceau was motivated probably by his exasperation with the Italians whose claims in Turkey were now challenged by Greece. The significance of this deplorable adventure is that in 1921 and 1922 conflicts over Turkey poisoned relations between Britain and France. The nadir was the meeting between Lord Curzon and Poincaré, on 19 September 1922, which reduced Curzon to tears. He had to be led from the room, complaining, 'I can't bear that horrid little man.' Nothing was at stake for either party that remotely merited the ill-feeling which developed over Turkey until sanity was restored by the Treaty of Lausanne of July 1923.[13]

A similar pattern emerges in Anglo-French relations about the Arab lands liberated from Ottoman rule. The starting point for discussion of this question has to be the Sykes-Picot accord of 16 May 1916 which divided the Ottoman Empire up between Britain, France and Russia, with provision for independent Arab states and an international zone in Palestine. The agreement was needed before Britain could embark on an offensive from Egypt, because France had traditional if vague claims to a protective role to what the French called 'integral Syria', which went all the way from the Taurus mountains in Cilicia to Sinai, and from the Mediterranean coast far east into the desert. There were complicated divisions into zones of direct rule and zones where Britain and France would 'advise' Arab rulers. The essence of the division was that Britain got Mesopotamia (much of modern Iraq), while France got modern Lebanon and Syria and the Mosul area. Matters were further complicated by British promises to the Arab rulers who revolted against Turkish rule, and the Balfour Declaration of November 1917 in favour of 'a national home for the Jewish people in Palestine.' The position in January 1919 was that in spite of contradictory British promises, both Britain and France still regarded themselves as being bound by the Sykes-Picot accord. But Britain wished to get French agreement to change it. Lloyd George wanted to put Palestine in the British zone, and also to get Mosul, where it was hoped that oil would be found. At an informal, undocumented meeting in London in December 1918, Clemenceau agreed to these changes, with the proviso that France would be entitled to a share of the Mosul oil and for British support on other matters. It was not recorded what this was to be, in precise terms, but Clemenceau declared subsequently that Lloyd George had gone back on his word. Lloyd George complained more that once, and in the most insulting terms, that the British army had conquered the Middle East without French help and thus French claims to Syria were spurious. To which Clemenceau could reply that the war effort of the two allies had to be regarded as a whole. Diversion of British military power to the Middle East had weakened the Allied effort on the Western Front. This did not alter the fact that in 1919 the Middle East was controlled by the British army, including the areas promised to France in 1916. The problem of reconciling this division of the spoils of war with Wilsonian national self-determination was solved by the mandate concept devised by Smuts. In the end, by the final agreement arrived at between Britain and France at San Remo in April 1920, the British and French zones were fixed as they had been by the Sykes-Picot agreement modified by the bargain between Lloyd George and Clemenceau in December 1918.

But this was only after quarrels of Homeric proportions while Britain tried to reduce the French share, arguing that the Arabs were happy to accept Britain as a tutelary power, but not France. One of the high points of this confrontation was at the meeting of the Council of Four on 20 March, not fully documented as this was before the interpreter Mantoux was called in. Further violent confrontation between Clemenceau and Lloyd George followed in May when the latter refused to withdraw British troops from Syria as had been agreed. Finally Clemenceau simply refused to discuss Syria any longer, complaining that he had made concession after concession. He told Poincaré: *It would not be possible to show more bad faith than Lloyd George. He has made me the most marvellous promises in the world and now he is going back on them all.*[14] The diatribe continues for two pages of Poincaré's diary. Paradoxically it was at this time that the French colonial party, with support from Berthelot in the Quai d'Orsay, were accusing Clemenceau of betraying French interests in Syria because of his obsessive Anglophilia.

It would not be possible to show more bad faith than Lloyd George. He has made me the most marvellous promises in the world and now he is going back on them all.
CLEMENCEAU TO POINCARÉ

We have already followed this conflict from the armistice to the summer of 1919, at which point it was far from resolution. An important stage was reached on 12–13 September 1919. Clemenceau talked with Lloyd George's assistant Philip Kerr on 12 September, and with the Prime Minister himself on 13 September. Kerr reported Clemenceau's position to Lloyd George in the following terms: 'He personally was not particularly concerned with the Near East. France, however, had always played a great part there, and from the

Turkey and the Near East 1923

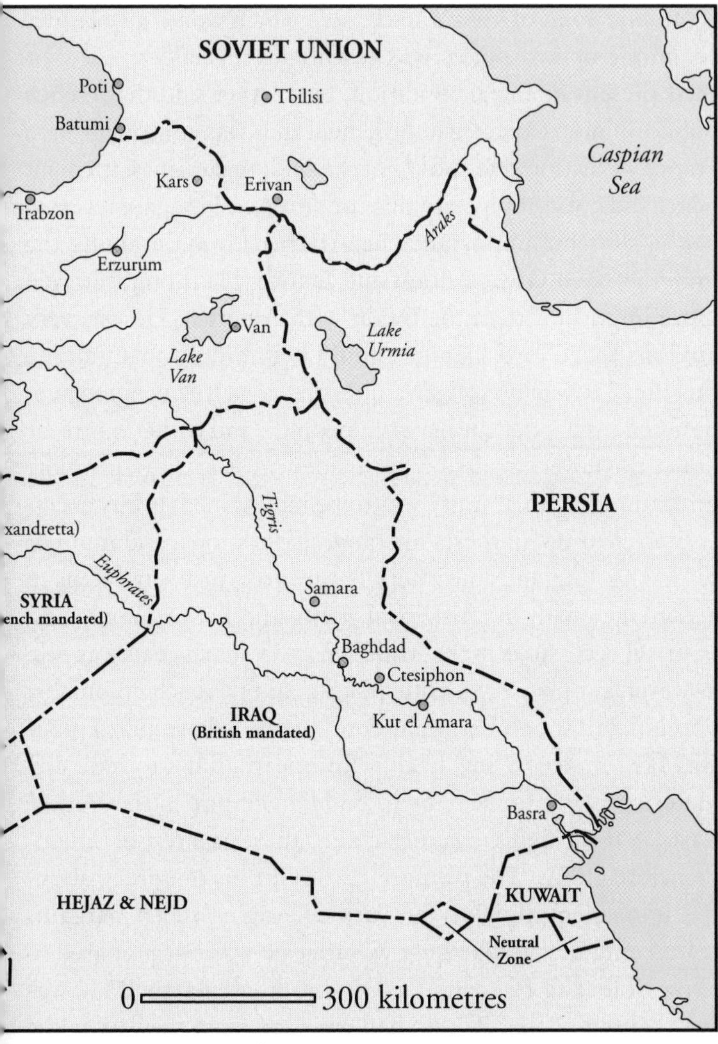
SOVIET UNION
Poti
Tbilisi
Batumi
Caspian Sea
Kars
Erivan
Trabzon
Araks
Erzurum
Van
Lake Urmia
Lake Van
Tigris
PERSIA
xandretta)
Euphrates
Samara
SYRIA
ench mandated)
Baghdad
Ctesiphon
IRAQ
(British mandated)
Kut el Amara
Basra
KUWAIT
HEJAZ & NEJD
Neutral Zone
0
300 kilometres

economic point of view a settlement which would give France economic opportunities was essential, especially in view of their present financial condition. He further said that French public opinion expected a settlement that was consonant with France's position. He could not, he said, make any settlement which did not comply with this condition ... He again reverted to the supreme importance he attached to maintaining the unity between Great Britain and France. He thought it even more important than the union with America. He was very anxious that Lloyd George should help him in maintaining this unity. It was no longer a question of securing agreement between monarchs but between peoples, and if this was to be done, the governments of both sides must actively promote understanding ... If unity was to be maintained, it was necessary to clear up all these outstanding questions, and in order to do this England must help France to a just settlement in accordance with her historical rights and her economic and political necessities in the Middle East.' Clemenceau was not, however, simply a reluctant spokesman of French colonialist opinion. Although he might continue to believe that France was far too deeply involved in European affairs to have any material reason for seeking to build an empire in the Middle East, he presented the French claims there as a test of Anglo-French relations. The primary reason for his obduracy about the implementation of the various Anglo-French bargains concerning the Middle East was that he was not prepared to allow France to be treated as a subordinate partner. He was very conscious that Britain had emerged from the war as the greatest military power in the world, while French military strength had been shattered. It was all the more important that France should not adopt the psychology of a defeated nation. This could best be achieved by standing up to British demands even while maintaining the alliance. If France were not to appear merely as a British satellite, he could not allow Lloyd George unilaterally to change the terms of the Anglo-French bargain over the Middle East. But by September 1919 Lloyd George was forced to accept that British military resources were being massively overstretched. British troops were withdrawn from Syria, although without consultation and in a way that seemed designed to be as offensive as possible: until the last the British supported the Arabs under Feisal against the French. Then in October 1919 Feisal was abandoned and told to make the best terms he could with France. He met Clemenceau on 20 October who told him that he was simply a British agent. Thus by the autumn of 1919 France controlled Syria, now divided into Lebanon and Syria, and temporarily Cilicia, soon to be handed back to a resurgent Turkey. At talks in London in December Clemenceau assured Lloyd George that: *My great desire is to do everything possible to eliminate friction between Great Britain and France.*[15]

This policy he brought to a successful conclusion, in diplomatic terms, in the autumn of 1919. No doubt he had been wise to postpone decisions until this time. As time went on it became easier to organise a large French army to occupy Syria, although only in the spring of 1920 were enough troops made available for the conquest of Syria after the Arab revolt. By that time it was being increasingly brought home to Lloyd George that ambitious plans for British control of the Middle East would require military backing quite out of proportion to its possible strategic advantages. British troops were withdrawn, handing over to the French in the Lebanon, the coastal zone, and to the Arabs in Damascus and the Syrian interior. It was only a matter of time before the Arabs either accepted French control or had it forced on them by conquest.

Clemenceau and Feisal negotiated in October and November, finally coming to an agreement formalised in a letter to Feisal of 17 December. Syria was to be a French protectorate, or, to use the new League of Nations term, mandate. In practice this would mean the same sort of tight administrative control that France exercised in its other protectorates, something very different from what President Wilson had envisaged when he agreed to the principle of mandates. The result was a revolt, which forced Feisal in March 1920 to repudiate the agreement and proclaim Syrian independence, shortly before the San Remo conference agreed to the French mandate in Syria. By July the Syrian revolt was crushed and the French were firmly in control. Clemenceau had been responsible for the addition of a large new colony to the already extensive French empire. This was not a very wise move: as he was well aware, France was already overstretched.

The British and French mandates were in essentials the same as had been agreed a year earlier, with the same provision for a French share in the oil of Mosul. The bad feeling between Britain and France on these matters throughout 1919 had produced virtually no change in their relative positions in the Middle East. Lloyd George's duplicity and high-handedness had simply made Clemenceau more determined to defend French claims in Syria which he had admitted from the first he attached no importance to.

9

Defence of the Treaty, July–December 1919

On 30 June the Treaty was presented to the French Chamber of Deputies for ratification, along with the Anglo-American guarantee treaties. The process in France was not as automatic as in Britain, where international treaties were covered by the royal prerogative. Although there was no question in France, unlike the United States, of the legislature failing to ratify the Treaty, it involved lengthy consideration, first in the special commissions set up for that purpose by the Chamber and the Senate, and then in the Chamber and Senate themselves. Clemenceau presented it to the Chamber in a speech on 30 June 1919, in which he referred back to his memories of 1870–1. One of his themes was that, in contrast to the disunity of that time, it was now vital that France should maintain its national unity. He said *general peace will only be the false mirage of a day if we are not capable of living at peace with ourselves.* He continued *the man who had organised after 1871 the final savage attack (that is Bismarck) had encouraged our republic in the hope that it would bring weakness, discord and national disintegration. So little did he understand liberty. The experiment that he wished for developed freely for half a century. His own people, chained to the chariot of its warlord beneath the yoke of human subservience can now recognise the result of the experiment. History has spoken.*[1]

In this speech Clemenceau returned to a theme that he had developed many times before, most clearly in the speech that he made in defence of Zola during the Dreyfus Affair. It is worth quoting as a fuller expression of the difference which he saw exemplified in the conflict between a German polity based on the rule of the army and militarism and the liberal democracy of the Entente states, whether constitutional monarchies or republics. He had argued in 1898 that the defenders of Dreyfus were not, as their opponents said, attacking the army: *There was nothing more absurd than the accusation that they were insulting the army. They honoured the army by requiring it to respect the law … For the last twenty-five years France has been engaged in a double enterprise, which seems contradictory to some. We were defeated … and we sought first to rebuild the military might of France. That is necessary, because unless we are first of all our own masters, there can be no civil law, no right or justice. And then we had a second idea, the idea of freeing ourselves from all despotisms, personal and oligarchic, and of founding in our country a democratic society, based on liberty and equality. Then the question arose of whether these*

Marcel Proust, in his famous novel, said that the attitudes of high society towards Clemenceau in 1918–19 illustrated one of the laws of time and memory that he had explored: he noted that for young people memory of the Dreyfus Affair persisted vaguely for them from what their fathers had said, so that if one told them that Clemenceau had been a Dreyfusard, they would reply: 'Oh no, impossible, you are mistaken, he was absolutely on the other side.'[2]

two ends were contradictory. The principle of civil society is right, liberty, justice ... But soldiers have no function except that of defending the principle of civil society. If, absorbed by the idea of national defence, civil society abandoned itself to military servitude, then we might still have some soil to defend, but we would have abandoned everything which had up to now given France her glory and renown in the world, ideas of liberty and justice.[3]

His speech was greeted with enormous enthusiasm by the Chamber, and the Treaty was handed over to the Commission for more detailed examination. The Commission included several important politicians who strongly resented their exclusion from the process of negotiation, and who were now determined to have their say. Louis Barthou was unanimously elected rapporteur-general of the Commission, and thus had the task of drafting the report submitted to the Chamber by it. Barthou had already expressed in the press his view that Germany was being treated too leniently, but he was a Centre-Right politician, not an extremist. Thus his report advocated ratification of the Treaty, but criticised some aspects of it, particularly with regard to security. Barthou was also doubtful about the Anglo-American treaties of guarantee, and had said as much directly to Clemenceau in the committee meeting of 17 July. But in the end he thought that the Treaty, with all its imperfections, should be ratified. When Louis Marin, a more right-wing political figure, moved that ratification should be deferred until the American Senate had voted in favour of the treaty of guarantee, and the treaties with the other enemy powers had been concluded, Barthou spoke against him and ensured his defeat. The Commission voted by a great majority for ratification. Barthou's report 'offered a mixture of praise and muted criticism'. He accepted that

Clemenceau had had no alternative but to abandon France's demand for permanent separation of the Rhineland from the rest of Germany, in the face of the adamant refusal of Britain and the United States to agree. But the value of the treaties of guarantee remained uncertain.[4]

In the debate in the Chamber Barthou developed these points more openly than in the text of the report itself. He pointed out that the United States might not ratify the Treaty, and that in that case the British guarantee would also evaporate. It was primarily these criticisms from Barthou that Clemenceau addressed when he spoke in the Chamber in defence of the Treaty on 24–25 September, leaving it to his ministers to answer criticism of particular parts of it. But on 24 September Barthou demanded an answer from the Prime Minister himself. It had already become apparent that the United States Senate might not ratify either the Treaty of Versailles or the treaty of guarantee. Barthou complained that, in that case, France would have lost the guarantee of security for which it had agreed to surrender its claim to the Rhine frontier. Clemenceau replied, no doubt disguising his real opinions, that he was sure that the American Senate would ratify the treaties. In any case, he said, if ratification did not occur, a special clause provided France with a means of ensuring its security: *There is an article, which I myself got adopted, which provides that in that case, we will make new arrangements concerning the Rhine. As a result, we are safeguarded in that respect, and everything has been provided for.*[5]

This declaration, which implied that France had a unilateral right to prolong the occupation of the Rhineland, was highly misleading, and was not accepted by Barthou. The relevant clause stated that 'if at that date the guarantees against unprovoked aggression were not considered sufficient by the Allied and Associated governments, the evacuation of the occupying troops may be delayed to the extent regarded as necessary for the purpose of obtaining the required guarantees'.

Lloyd George had strenuously, and successfully, resisted the much more sweeping wording first proposed by the French, which would have given France alone the right to postpone evacuation. But Clemenceau and Tardieu implied that France alone did have the right, under this clause, to prolong the occupation. Clemenceau's main speech in defence of the Treaty was made the next day, 25 September. He did not discuss it in detail. Indeed he said that the great mistake of earlier speakers had been to present detailed criticism of particular sections of the Treaty. He knew that it was imperfect. But the war had been fought by a coalition, and the Treaty must express the lowest common denominator of the views of all the partners. It was easy to see how many details could be improved on. But the important thing was to look at the Treaty as a whole, not in a carping, critical, negative spirit, but to see what could be made of it. This theme he developed with great eloquence in his peroration.

He declared: *The treaty, with all its complex clauses, will only be worth what you are worth: it will be what you make it … What you are going to vote today is not even a beginning, it is a beginning of a beginning. The ideas it contains will grow and bear fruit. You have won the power to impose them on a defeated Germany. We are told that she will revive. All the more reason not to show her that we fear her … M Marin went to the heart of the question, when he turned to us and said in despairing tomes, 'You have reduced us to a policy of vigilance'. Yes M Marin, do you think that one could make a treaty which would do away with the need for vigilance among the nations of Europe who only yesterday were pouring out their blood in battle? Life is a perpetual struggle in war, as in peace … That struggle cannot be avoided. Yes, we must have vigilance, we must have a great deal of vigilance. I cannot say for how many centuries the crisis which has begun will continue. Yes, this treaty will bring us burdens, troubles, miseries, difficulties, and that will continue for long years.*[6]

'From the belief that essentially the old order does not change, being based on human nature, which is always the same, and from a consequent scepticism of all that class of doctrine which the League of Nations stands for, the policy of France and of Clemenceau followed logically … He sees the issue in terms of France and Germany, not of humanity and of European civilisation struggling forward towards a new order. The war has bitten into his consciousness somewhat differently from ours and he neither expects nor hopes that we are at the threshold of a new age.'

KEYNES ON CLEMENCEAU'S POLITICAL PSYCHOLOGY[7]

These passages elevated the debate to the emotional level attained by all his great wartime speeches. Whatever the criticism of points of detail, there could be no denying that he had drawn out the historical significance of the Treaty in a way no other speaker had attempted. Over the next 20 years his insistence on the need for France to continue its wartime effort was to take on steadily more significance. The great mistake, not only of France, but of all the wartime allies, was to believe the Treaty could preserve for ever the balance of forces achieved in 1918. It was not a mistake Clemenceau made. The Treaty was ratified by 372 votes to 53, the opposition consisting of rather more than half the Socialist deputies, of Franklin-Bouillon, a persistent Radical critic of the government from the time of its formation, and of the right-wing deputy Louis Marin, whose views Clemenceau had seized on in his speech.

On 11 October Clemenceau spoke again in defence of the Treaty in the Senate. Here the persistent opposition of the Chamber was absent, and ratification was voted unanimously. He made many of the same points as in his speech in the Chamber but in a less combative, and more philosophical spirit. A main theme of this speech was to combat those who advocated splitting up Germany. He declared that to attempt to destroy national unity, which depended on feeling, by institutional devices, would be self-defeating. France must therefore find a way of living alongside 60 million Germans. He ended with some general reflections on what he had, in 1891, referred to as the rise of the Fourth Estate. The bourgeoisie, he said, like the aristocracy of the *ancien régime*, had failed as a ruling class, and now it was the turn of the working class to seek to become a ruling class. This led him back to the need for national unity, and a final plea for a demographic revolution: *The treaty does not state that France will have many children, but it is the first thing that should have been written there. For if France does not have large families, it will be in vain that you put all the finest clauses in the treaty, that you take away all the German guns, France will be lost because there will be no more French.*[8]

It is ironic that he chose this subject for the closing remarks of his last parliamentary speech, for the 20 years that followed saw the birth-rate fall to a phenomenally low level. There could hardly have been a more pointed indication that France was not prepared to follow the arduous road to national greatness pointed out for it by Clemenceau in these speeches. Precisely what he feared did take place. The great effort of the war had been too much. National willpower and energy had been sapped in a fundamental way, so that the continuing German challenge was not to be met by an ever vigilant and self-confident France.

In contrast to Britain where a new parliament had already been elected by December 1918, the French Chamber of Deputies, which had been elected only four months before the outbreak of war, continued until the autumn of 1919. Apart from any other considerations, this delay was made inevitable by the decision to adopt a new electoral system. The new system, which was only used in 1919 and 1924, was adopted in response to the advocates of proportional representation, who had long been campaigning for a change in the traditional two-ballot system. They had, however, been defeated before 1914 in part because of Clemenceau's determined opposition. In 1919 he declared that he was too preoccupied with other matters to devote time to this. The system adopted was very different from a truly proportional one, almost the opposite in fact. It provided for multi-member constituencies, which usually consisted of a department where an electoral list which won a majority of the votes took all the seats. Proportional representation only applied if no list gained an absolute majority. So the drawing up of a coalition list that could win a majority of votes was at a high premium. In this the intransigence of the Socialists put the Left at a disadvantage. The Socialist party refused to participate in any coalition, seeking as they were to maintain their own party unity in the face of the challenge resulting from the Bolshevik revolution. This also left the Radicals in an isolated position, unless they agreed to join Centre and Centre-Right lists. In the new political atmosphere the moderate Republicans, who had usually looked for support from the left rather than the right before 1914, joined with the Right to draw up many of the departmental lists. This resulted in the triumph of the *Bloc National*, a coalition of Right and Centre, and the overwhelming defeat of Socialists and Radicals. The arbitrary working of the new electoral system was more responsible for the swing to the Right than a change in the sentiments of the electorate.

Clemenceau's presiding over the *Bloc National*'s electoral triumph indicated the extent of his move to the Right, which had not been so evident before the election. In the old Chamber of Deputies, the great majority of Radicals had reluctantly supported the government. The political situation had been similar to that during Clemenceau's first ministry, in which the support of the bulk of the Radicals had been retained, with a minority left-wing opposition made up of Radical-Socialists and Socialists. However the success of the *Bloc National* under his patronage was another stage in his evolution to the Right. Mandel and Tardieu, political disciples of Clemenceau, entered politics as members of the Right. He himself had not taken much part in the election campaign, seeing himself as more a national figure, than the leader of a partisan majority. The result was that Mandel and Tardieu encountered difficulties when seeking to use Clemenceau's name to help them to create a new right-wing party.

Clemenceau was only prepared to intervene twice. Once was during the November election campaign in Strasbourg in 1919, and the second time was his decision to stand for election as President. At Strasbourg, Clemenceau gave his accolade to the programme and men of the *Bloc National*, with Millerand at his side. His speech appealed for national unity, and the safeguarding of the achievements of victory through constant effort and vigilance. He repeated the defence of the peace treaty that he had given in his parliamentary speeches. He also supported some specific proposals of the *Bloc National*, such as the welcoming of Catholics if they sincerely abandoned their reactionary ties. He stressed the need for strong government, declaring this could only be achieved by the creation of a strong and determined governmental majority, and not by constitutional reform. The only constitutional reform he envisaged was decentralisation with representative assemblies in the provinces: he said he had planned this during his first ministry, and that his proposals had been shelved and were still in the files of the administration. He also spoke of the need to encourage equality through social reforms and the need to stop the conflict between Labour and Capital. His condemnation of Bolshevism, however, was his most striking point. He said that it aimed to destroy the Republic and to put in its place the bloody dictatorship of anarchy. This implied wholesale condemnation of the Socialist party for its refusal to break with its extremist elements.

Clemenceau's prestige, combined with the electoral system and the lack of unity of the Left, resulted in a sweeping victory for the *Bloc National*. The Chamber of Deputies was now the most right-wing since 1871. Mordacq reported that Clemenceau was disconcerted by the extent of the move to the Right, and that he refused to make any commitments when he met the new Chamber in December 1919 and was asked about his general policy. He was given a vote of confidence, with the Socialists opposing. Clemenceau had up to this point given no indication that he might stand as President himself: on the contrary, he had said more than once that he only wished to complete his wartime task by ensuring the ratification of the peace treaties. He would then, he said, be happy to retire to private life. This would seem sensible for a man of 78 who had just experienced two exhausting years.

However, he gave in to pressure from Mandel and agreed to allow his name to go forward as a presidential candidate, believing he was certain to be elected. It was only on 20 January 1920 that he allowed Mandel to state publicly that he would be prepared to serve if elected. Why did he decide to stand for the presidency? For most of the life of the Third Republic the president was little more than a ceremonial figurehead, but Poincaré, the most important politician to be president during the Third Republic, had tried to develop a stronger role for the office. He had enjoyed some success until Clemenceau had arrived as his prime minister. Thus with the roles reversed, and Clemenceau as president with all the prestige of the Father of Victory, he could hope to play a more prominent role than Poincaré had done. One important power was the right of the president to choose the prime minister, and Clemenceau might have been able to appoint a loyal supporter in that role, so that they could jointly weld the *Bloc National* into a coherent political force. This plan appealed to ambitious men like Tardieu and Mandel, who had tied their fortunes to Clemenceau, and whose retirement was to leave them out of office. There was a widespread feeling among political circles at this time that France needed a stronger governmental system, with or without constitutional change. This was represented by the election of Poincaré and then of Millerand as presidents. Clemenceau's decision to stand is made explicable by this context. However there were many obstacles: against it were all constitutional conventions: presidents who attempted to direct politics provoked resentment in Parliament.

In fact Clemenceau was not elected. He was rejected in

favour of the colourless Deschanel (although he obtained an ironic revenge several months later when Deschanel had a nervous breakdown and had to resign). He might in fact have been elected had he fought for the post, but he wished to be acclaimed as a national symbol. The decisive vote came in the preliminary meeting of the republican caucus. Clemenceau had been highly indignant when Poincaré had refused to accept the decision of such a caucus, in 1913, and had gone on to win with the support of the Right. No doubt this was one reason why Clemenceau refused to follow a similar course of action, although by now the old division between republican and non-republican deputies had little meaning. The caucus was open to all who wished to attend, and the votes were 389 for Clemenceau against 408 for Deschanel. A large proportion of the *Bloc National* were Catholics who did not support Clemenceau because of his anti-clericalism, and others like Briand were personally hostile, arguing that as president he would reduce the power of Parliament, upsetting the balance of the constitution. Clemenceau at first could not believe the news brought him by his *chef de cabinet*. When it

ARISTIDE BRIAND (1872–1932) Although Briand began his ministerial career alongside Clemenceau in 1906, and serving in his first ministry, from 1917 the two men were at opposite poles. Briand was the archetype of a Third Republican politician, holding office with very few breaks from 1906 to 1917, and from 1921 to 1932, often as prime minister. At first more concerned with domestic affairs, notably religious, from 1915 on he was primarily involved with foreign policy. In 1916 to 1917 he formulated an ambitious programme of war aims, but afterwards was the advocate of conciliation and peace. Excluded from any role in the negotiations of 1919, he was in Clemenceau's eyes, even more responsible than Poincaré for failing to uphold the terms of the Treaty. During his long reign as Foreign Minister from 1925 to 1932 he negotiated the Locarno treaties of 1925, endorsed the Dawes and Young Plans on reparations, and made friendly overtures to the German foreign minister Stresemann.

finally registered, he said; *That's it: I do not wish to be voted for tomorrow.* He remained adamant, despite the fact that he could very well have been elected by the full National Assembly. He explained that he did not want to be elected by a tiny minority, and that to negotiate with the Allies he needed the prestige and authority that virtually unanimous acclaim would have provided. He felt the defeat deeply as a personal affront, and from this time his comments on the men and affairs of his native country acquired a new bitterness.[9]

Clemenceau's entourage have claimed that the failure to elect him as President led to failures of French diplomacy in the 1920s, arguing that he would have been able to prevent the rapid dissolution of the Versailles settlement. Clemenceau himself also complained several times about the subsequent destruction of his diplomatic achievement. He argued that he would have been able to maintain the entente with Britain, and maybe also with the United States, while enforcing all of the provisions of the Treaty. Instead those in power allowed Franco-British relations to become very bad, and did not even hang on to French rights under the Treaty. He declared: *I assure you that if I had been in power in 1920, at the time of the occupation of Frankfurt, I would never have accepted the English not being at our side, and they would have finished by coming. But, instead of being open with them, we have tried to show that we could manage without them. To be completely open would have been the only way to combat the hostile policy of Lloyd George: in the face of such an attitude on our part, he would not in the end have been supported by the English people, who have always been loyal to us.* He similarly condemned Poincaré's 1923 occupation of the Ruhr as a sign of the breach between French and English policy.[10]

These comments seem to show a great deal of wishful

thinking. They were reported by Mordacq in detail, and have been reported as well-founded judgements by some biographers. They lament the 'sabotage' of the Treaty of Versailles after Clemenceau's retirement. It is not clear, however, how Clemenceau could have achieved the *tour de force* of combining an even more rigorous policy towards Germany than that of his successors, with the maintenance of the entente with England. Under Lloyd George or any other prime minister, the British were not prepared to be carried in the wake of a French chauvinistic anti-German policy. There is no reason to think that with Clemenceau as President there would have been different developments. His last remarks to the cabinet, before handing over power in January 1920, were that he had wished to restore French self-confidence: *We must show the world the extent of our victory, and we must take up the mentality and habits of a victorious people, which once more takes its place at the head of Europe. But all that will now be placed in jeopardy ... it will take less time and less thought to destroy the edifice so patiently and painfully erected than it took to complete it. Poor France. The mistakes have begun already.*[11]

Clemenceau at home at St Vincent sur Jard in the 1920s.

III

The Legacy

10

After 1920

As soon as the presidential election was over, Clemenceau resigned as prime minister, and remained away from the political scene for well over a year. On a visit to his old friend the painter Claude Monet at his country house at Giverny on the day of the election, he had told him that he intended to visit Egypt. Only two weeks later he set off, and penetrated as far as the swamps of the Nile in Sudan. He returned to France on 21 April. He abstained from any political comments, and after spending some of the summer months at Vichy he then set off for the Far East, in September, only returning in March 1921, after visiting Singapore, the Dutch East Indies and British India. Despite arduous rail journeys in India his health benefited from the long voyages by sea, and he was much fitter on his return home. He visited Oxford in June 1921 to receive an honorary degree and to visit many English friends. Initially he refused to meet Lloyd George but eventually agreed to do so. This meeting was not a success, and Clemenceau reproached the British prime minister with becoming France's enemy the moment peace was signed. Lloyd George replied, 'well, was that not always our traditional policy?' The exchange was jocular, but Clemenceau, brooding over the evolution of British policy, took it with utter seriousness, rejoicing later at the news of Lloyd George's fall from power, saying: *As for France, it is a real enemy who disappears. Lloyd George did not hide it: at my last visit to London he cynically admitted it.*[1]

There was nothing sentimental about Clemenceau's pro-English policy, although he had many English friends. He only sought an entente with England because power politics necessitated it. A friend who went with him to India, Piétri, reports that he said that he did not like the egoism of England; personally he had nothing to learn about that: he had suffered from it enough during his discussions with Lloyd George. He knew all about it, but he said that they have no choice: whether they wished it or not, they had to remember that that they were in no position to quarrel with England.

During autumn 1921 he again started to consider playing a political role, telling Mordacq that he believed he had a duty to support those who had helped him in the creation of the Treaty, and were now trying to defend it, although he himself did not wish to participate once more in the political struggle. He helped Tardieu to gather financial support by setting up a newspaper, *L'Echo National*, with Tardieu as political editor, and himself named as founder. However, publication ceased after two years, and Clemenceau disappointed expectations by not writing for it. Before long he was expressing dissatisfaction with the policies of Tardieu, though not as strongly as he condemned some other former colleagues. This tendency to see political betrayal in all the actions of his former colleagues led to his gradual isolation from them. In 1922 he went on a lecture tour speaking in all the main north-eastern cities of the United States. His speeches defended French policy, especially with regard to war debts and reparations, and condemned the withdrawal of the United States from the alliance. He was well received by large and appreciative audiences, but his views made little impact on the American public. Their policy of isolation was not to be influenced by the old French statesman.[2] He was now resigned to the ending of his active political career, and took only one more initiative, his open letter of August 1926 to President Coolidge. This concerned French war debts to America, and protested against the American insistence that France repay all debts contracted during and after the war. This had no effect on American policy.

He now returned to the intellectual pursuits, writing and publishing, which had at intervals in his busy political life always attracted him. These included two biographies, one of Demosthenes and a moving tribute to his long friendship with Monet. Clemenceau had a lifelong interest in art, and was said to have been an excellent guide round exhibitions but serious aesthetic analysis was really beyond his scope. Most of his time in the mid-1920s was taken up by a massive two-volume work of philosophical speculation, *Au Soir de la Pensée*, which ranged over political, historical and scientific subjects, an ambitious work, remarkable for a man of his age.

His intellect and energy were still impressive, and his immense curiosity about the world remained undiminished, and there are many passages of vigorous writing, but the fact is that the work is 'prolix, repetitive and badly organised'. The digressions and footnotes are often among the most interesting components, rather than the main argument. Clemenceau's basic position was still that imbibed from his father, that of 19th-century materialism. Even in the fields he knew well, evolution and biology, he was defending outdated theorists like Lamarck. The most thorough evaluation of the work commented: 'With an almost sentimental tenacity he clung to the mechanism of another century, and rejected the more flexible doctrines of contemporary materialists. He never wavered in his loyalty to the philosophy of the ideologues fashioned by Diderot, Helvetius and d'Holbach. Even when he incorporated the findings of 20th-century scientists, he merely reinforced his beliefs from an older materialism.'[3]

Clemenceau spent his last seven years in writing these books, and living either in his modest apartment in Paris, or in St Vincent sur Jard, in the Vendée. This was a remote village by the sea where he had a simple holiday cottage and took great pleasure in making a garden, and succeeding in growing roses which was generally believed to be impossible in such sandy ground. He had taken the cottage in 1921, spending most of his summers there, looked after by his faithful servants, Brabant the chauffeur, Albert the valet and Clotilde, his cook *cum* housekeeper.

The last months of Clemenceau's life were devoted to the composition of *Grandeurs et Misères d'une Victoire*. He had several times declared that he was not going to write his memoirs, but he reacted to the publication of *Le Mémorial de Foch*. This was a posthumous work, compiled by Raymond Recouly, consisting largely of attacks on Clemenceau. Foch claimed that he had opposed his promotion to the supreme command during the war, and than attacked his policy at the time of the peace settlement. Clemenceau's book initially was to refute these charges, but it became a more general defence of his policy during the war and at the peacemaking and into a diatribe against his successors who had allowed the Treaty to be destroyed. It would not be fair to judge it as a finished product as he only had time to produce a first draft. However the main lines of his argument are clear enough. They are that the terms which he had managed to negotiate were enough to protect France's dearly gained victory. But they had been eroded from the very first. He was especially scornful of Poincaré, who had bitterly criticised him for not achieving better terms and had then, as prime minister from 1922–4, and again from 1926–8, had allowed the emasculation of the terms that he had achieved. He drafted six chapters on the various mutilations of the Treaty beginning with the failure of ratification by the United States. His argument was that as he had abandoned the demand for a separate Rhineland specifically because of the offer of the Anglo-American guarantees, when those guarantees were abandoned, France should have reopened the question of the Rhineland. Instead of that, *not a sign, not a word*. France simply let the matter drop. His diatribe continued with the failure to collect reparations, ending with the effective replacement of the reparations commission with committees presided over by American bankers. This meant that France received only a small proportion of what had been promised in reparations, while the Americans were insisting on the repayment of their wartime loans. He included in his book the text of the open letter he had sent to President Coolidge on 9 August 1926, in protest at this.

He continued with criticism of the treaties signed at Locarno in December 1925. These treaties were, first, a treaty between Germany, France, Belgium, Britain and Italy, by which all parties guaranteed the Franco-Belgian-German borders, and the demilitarised status of the Rhineland. Secondly there were also treaties between France and Poland and Czechoslovakia, and between Germany and its eastern neighbours, but these were not signed by Britain, and did not specifically guarantee existing frontiers. In other words Germany implicitly reserved the right to change these frontiers. Britain stated that it was out of the question for it to guarantee the Eastern Frontiers. This is ironical in view of what brought Britain to declare war on Germany in 1939. Clemenceau saw the significance of this part of Locarno, declaring it to be a *mutilation* of Versailles. He also thought that it was a *mutilation* because it placed Germany on an equal footing with the victors of 1919, and paved the way for its entry into the League of Nations. For Briand and Austen Chamberlain, the British and French statesmen who negotiated the new settlement, this was precisely the point. Locarno reiterated what Germany had signed at Versailles, but it could not be called a 'Diktat'. This time the German government had willingly and freely signed. Of course, this made no difference in 1936, when Hitler invaded the Rhineland, and tore up 'the scrap of paper' as Clemenceau said would happen.

The next chapter attacked German failure to disarm, while France herself in reality disarmed. In a chapter on the organisation of frontier defence he pointed out what turned out in 1940 to be a crucial failure leaving France open to invasion through Belgium. But *Grandeur and Misery* was not mainly a technical discussion of detail. It was an appeal, above all in the last chapters, 'Peace in retreat' and 'The unknown soldier', to the people of France to reassert themselves to defend the security that had been bought by so much blood on the battlefield, and to resist the continued German efforts to dismantle the safeguards of the Treaty. He saw France and its wartime allies in the place of the Greek city states whose divisions allowed them, with all their higher civilisation, to be defeated by the barbarian king Philip of Macedon. Although he found it difficult to see any reason for optimism:

I cannot resign myself to the thought that our last word has been said. He continued: *It is only too clear that logic should lead us to the most sombre predictions. I would like to avoid them. But I search the horizon in vain for a sign of revival ... I want to believe that civilisation will triumph over savagery and that alone forces me to exclude Germany from a life of mutual dignity as long as she continues to base her energetic reactions on the lie that she did not will the war ... If Germany obsessed by its traditional militarism, persists in its Deutschland uber alles, then let the die be cast. We will take up again the terrible war where we left off. We must have the courage to prepare for it, instead of letting ourselves be weakened from conference to conference by lies that deceive nobody. At the moment, Germany is arming and France is disarming.* Referring to the plebiscite in Germany, inspired by the nationalist opposition to the Young Plan, he pointed out what this revealed about German attitudes: *We can thus see, in the clear light of facts, the Germans armed for battle, while the French, heedless, applaud orators who announce violations of the peace treaty!* [4]

If Germany obsessed by its traditional militarism, persists in its *Deutschland uber alles*, then let the die be cast. We will take up again the terrible war where we left off. We must have the courage to prepare for it, instead of letting ourselves be weakened from conference to conference by lies that deceive nobody.

CLEMENCEAU

His last chapter began with an appeal to the unknown soldier, that body of that anonymous *poilu* buried under the Arc de Triomphe: *And now, unknown soldier of France, what do you say? What do you want, what do you do? Yes, you, modest, and noble creation of the popular mind, forever silent beneath the funeral stone, it is you I dare to question. It is not Foch's stories that haunt me. It is the future of France which is being decided at this moment …* These final pages were imbued with a profound pessimism about the future, although he still, hoping against his judgement, called on France and its future unknown soldier to react against the weak and defeatist leaders who had allowed the fruits of victory to be dissipated. *Every one of us is the little-known soldier of an unknown history: Even at this dangerous hour, perhaps our destiny is still in your hands. Even though neither Britain nor America are at our sides, England, struggling with all the problems created by its conquests, harassed at sea by America, and anxious about Japan, forgets too easily that our defeat would have left her at the mercy of Germany. Her soldiers are everywhere. How many, when the hour comes, will be present at Calais?*[5]

In his last words, he returned to the image of the ancient Greeks defending civilisation against the barbarity of the Orient, exemplified by the conquests of the rulers of Macedon, whose imperial tyranny was then continued by Rome. This was the parallel to *Germany seeking to recreate by the procedures of peace a German empire that it had failed to achieve by war … There are peoples who begin, and peoples who finish. France will be what the French deserve.*[6]

Clemenceau passed his 88th birthday on 28 September 1929, while composing this appeal to his fellow citizens. He had finished the first draft, but was unable to complete a revision before he succumbed to his final illness. After a few days in great agony he died on the night of 23/24 November 1929. He had always refused to agree to any sort of state funeral and his burial was to be of the simplest, involving only his family and a handful of his closest remaining friends.

Nevertheless the government organised a ceremony at the Arc de Triomphe for Sunday 1 December, but his family and friends refused to take part. Instead his body was taken to the Vendée, where it was to be buried, according to the terms of his will, not in any consecrated ground, but in a little wood on the ancestral farm at Le Colombier, near Mouchamps. His will read: *I wish to be buried at Le Colombier, by the side of my father. My body is to be carried to the burial place without any cortège or ceremony of any kind … Around the grave there is to be nothing but an iron railing, without any name, as for my father. Place in my coffin my walking stick with an iron knob, which was mine in my youth, and the little casket of goatskin in the left hand corner of my wardrobe, with inside it the little book that was placed there by the hand of my dear mother. Finally place there also the two little bunches of dried flowers, which are on the mantelpiece of the room by the garden …* [7]

All these instructions were carried out; the procession left Paris on 26 November after 2 a.m., so it was not surprising that only a small crowd watched its departure. At Le Colombier, the old farm, close to the village of Mouchamps, in the possession of the Clemenceau family from the early 18th century, there were only the peasants of the neighbourhood, members of the family, the few intimate friends who had accompanied the body from Paris, and a few press photographers. The grave remains unmarked, except for a bas-relief of Minerva by the sculptor

I wish to be buried at Le Colombier, by the side of my father. My body is to be carried to the burial place without any cortège or ceremony of any kind … Around the grave there is to be nothing but an iron railing, without any name, as for my father.

CLEMENCEAU

Sicard, which Clemenceau had had placed there. Remote and difficult to find, it is visited rarely.

There is a ridiculous legend that he had stipulated in his will that he be buried upright, on guard against the German invader. That it is without foundation was established by Winston Churchill, who had encountered it when preparing to write his essay on Clemenceau, published in *Great Contemporaries*. Churchill wrote to Clemenceau's daughter to check, and she replied with a denial.[8]

Clemenceau's final efforts had been to warn his fellow citizens of the *mutilations* that had already been perpetrated on the peace settlement, and of how successive political leaders had failed to defend the terms that had been won in the hard-fought negotiations of 1919. But his death came to the exact moment when developments were to bring about much more serious mutilations. In November 1929, in spite of the storm petrels that he had pointed out, the advancing storm itself was still only gathering in the distance. One thunder clap, of which there is no indication that he ever noticed it, was the collapse of share prices on the American stock exchange, on 'Black Thursday' 24 October, the following days of panic which triggered the Great Depression. Although France seemed at first to be immune, the financial links between the United States and Germany rapidly transmitted economic crises across the Atlantic. The important point is that in Germany the economic crisis soon produced a political crisis of which the outcome would be Hitler's dictatorship. Even before that event, the Allied occupation of the Rhineland had ended in 1930, and the attempt to collect reparations had in practice been abandoned with President Hoover's moratorium of 1931. Nevertheless, in strict military terms Germany was still helpless in the face of the French army, and would remain so at least until 1935. But demoralisation on the part of the victors of 1918, and their own disbelief in the terms they had imposed, meant that Hitler's abjuration of the disarmament clauses of the Treaty bought no reaction. Clemenceau's denunciation of the earlier failure to enforce the Treaty was shown to be prescient. Now that the German derogations were far more serious, the precedent had already been set. The turning point, of course, came in March 1936 when Hitler marched the German army into the demilitarised zone of the Rhineland, with no reaction. Perhaps it would have been different if the French plan for a separate buffer state had been adopted. As it was it seemed to be only a technical matter: the fact that it involved defiance of the Treaty of Versailles hardly mattered, now that the Treaty was regarded not as a bulwark against war, but as the source of conflict.

ooooo

Academic writing about the peace settlement over the last 40 years has achieved a high level of consensus on the crucial question of whether it was a flawed treaty that inevitably led to the Second World War. The consensus, in dramatic contrast to the views of those who are less informed, is that it did not lead inevitably to the second war. If the provisions of the Treaty had been upheld, they were sufficient to prevent Germany challenging the victors. At least until 1935 this could have been done without serious military engagement.

As David Stevenson has argued, the peace settlement 'could either have accommodated a lasting reconciliation with the new republican regime in Germany or ensured that it remained militarily harmless. The real tragedy of the inter-war years was that it did neither … The main reason for this tragedy was not that the treaty terms were impracticable or unjust. Nor did the Allies lack military strength. The more fundamental problem was their disunity'.[9]

Relating this verdict on the peace settlement to Clemenceau's endeavours is straightforward enough. His overriding aim, as he often stated in 1919 and afterwards, was to maintain the unity of the coalition that had defeated Germany. In order to maintain that unity, in 1919 and for the future, he sacrificed several desiderata, but managed by dint of persistent and tactful bargaining to preserve enough to defend the settlement into the future. It was in large part the result of this insistence that contrary to what Jacques Bainville argued, the peace was not too weak for what it contained which was harsh. Precisely the opposite: it could have been a peace of reconciliation if Germany had been willing to accept it, and if, as proved to be the case, Germany did not, it contained enough safeguards to allow for its enforcement. Clemenceau could claim, as he did in his final testament, that even without the Anglo-American guarantee treaties, France could herself have maintained the control over Germany that was necessary for French security. However, this was very much theoretical reasoning. The ink was hardly dry on the signatures to the Treaty before German resistance to its enforcement was met with accommodation and not with insistence on compliance. The foolish and symbolic affair of the trial of the ex-Kaiser demonstrated this as early as the autumn of 1919, when hints were given to the Dutch authorities that demands for his extradition were only formal. More serious was the fiasco of the German trials of those responsible for atrocities, and then the failure to collect more than token payment of reparations. Already by this stage the divergence between British and French attitudes was obvious. It became more so and more public, when Poincaré replaced Briand as prime minister in January 1922. France began to contemplate action to force German compliance with the Treaty even without British support. Whatever might have been theoretically possible, by 1924 unilateral French action to maintain the terms of the Treaty was abandoned. Franco-Belgian occupation of the Ruhr in 1923, in the face of outright British opposition, succeeded in breaking the German refusal to comply with the terms of the Treaty. But unilateral French action stopped at that point. Instead of building on this victory in a way that would have pre-empted further German intransigence at the expense of a complete breach with Britain, Millerand (the president of the Republic) and Poincaré (the prime minister), agreed to enter into negotiations involving not only British, French and Germans, but also American financiers. By the time the negotiations were seriously underway Poincaré and Millerand were out of office, and Herriot's left-wing government failed to play with any skill the hand of cards that it had been given by its predecessor. The result was the Dawes Plan of 1925, dramatically reducing both German reparations payments and the measures of control to enforce future payment. This was followed by the Locarno treaties, and German membership of the League of Nations. The option of interpreting the Treaty in a lenient way so as to seek reconciliation between the victors and Germany was followed from 1924 onwards. This went along with the maintenance of Allied unity as France abandoned the unilateral attempts to enforce the Treaty against German resistance that had been tried in 1922 and 1923. Unfortunately the search for reconciliation continued until 1938, long after revived German nationalism should have made the futility of such a course obvious. Thus it seems that Clemenceau's hope that he could combine maintenance of Allied unity with the minimum safeguards to protect France against its German neighbour's eventual resurgence, was doomed. If Britain could not see that rectification of the 'injustices' of Versailles would not produce a satisfied Germany, but an aggressive power seeking to overturn the defeat of 1918 and to avenge its supposed humiliation, the two aims were incompatible.

This was clear enough before Clemenceau's death, and became very much clearer in the ten years that followed. In the last years before the outbreak of war in 1939 French policy was the opposite of what he had advocated in his speeches defending the Treaty and in *Grandeur and Misery of Victory*. Instead of defending the safeguards that had been won in 1919, France, against its better judgement, abdicated to the British desire to conciliate and appease the German dictator.

Does this mean that Clemenceau was wrong to place so much reliance on the Anglo-Saxons, as his French critics argued? Surely not. France in 1919 was too weak to impose its own terms, and Clemenceau simply had to make an Allied peace, not a separate one. His critics could argue that he had been duped when the treaties of guarantee that had been promised by Wilson and Lloyd George did not materialise. He argued himself that his successors should have reopened the question when that happened. It is difficult to see what that could have achieved in 1922. But the guarantee treaties were always of symbolic rather than practical importance. It is obvious that Wilson thought that the proposed guarantee added nothing to the commitment undertaken by the Covenant of the League of Nations. Nor did Lloyd George consult with his military advisors, or investigate in any way what might have been involved in implementing the treaty of guarantee. Clemenceau himself stated that with or without a treaty, Britain would, in its own interests, intervene if Germany invaded France, as it had done without a treaty in 1914. As we know, even before that stage was reached, in 1939 Britain led the way in a joint Anglo-French declaration of war on Germany. The point of the guarantee was not to involve Britain in an eventual repeat of the First World War; it was to demonstrate a joint Anglo-French unity of purpose that would prevent such a repeat performance. Probably by April 1919 he had already come to realise that such a commitment on the part of the United States was unlikely, but it was a bitter blow when Lloyd George used the American failure to carry through the promised guarantee as a reason for backsliding himself.

With the hindsight achieved in the light of the Second World War it is easy to see that Clemenceau's assessment was correct. A repetition of the tragedy could only be avoided if Britain and France stood together to defend the settlement that had been imposed at Versailles in 1919. It would be best if the United States also stood where it had come to stand in 1917, but that was less likely and not absolutely essential. But it could have been reasonable to expect Britain to see before March 1939 that a firm alliance with France was more likely to prevent war than its actual policy of seeking to mediate between France and Germany.

Notes

Preface and Acknowledgements

1. F S Marston, *The Peace Conference of 1919, organisation and procedure* (Oxford University Press, London: 1944) pp 54–5, hereafter Marston, *Peace Conference*.
2. Georges Clemenceau, *Discours de Paix* (Plon, Paris: 1938) pp 88–9.
3. Alma Luckau, *The German Delegation at the Paris Peace Conference* (Columbia University Press, New York: 1941. New ed. Howard Fertig, 1971) pp 220–3, hereafter Luckau, *German Delegation*.
4. Strictly speaking, preliminaries of peace were signed at Versailles on 26 February 1871 between France and the German Empire, which had been proclaimed in the Hall of Mirrors on 18 January, even before the armistice; the terms were confirmed by the Treaty of Frankfurt on 10 May 1871.
5. Jacques Bainville, writing in the newspaper *L'Action Française* on 8 May 1919.

1: France in the World

1. General de Gaulle, *War memoirs: the Call to Honour, 1940–1942*, translated by Jonathan Griffin (Collins, London: 1955) p 9.
2. Jules Ferry, *Discours et Opinions, Vol. V*, p 172, quoted in David Robin Watson, *Georges Clemenceau, a political biography* (Eyre Methuen, London: 1974) p 95, hereafter Watson, *Georges Clemenceau.*
3. David R Watson, 'Clemenceau's contacts with England', *Diplomacy and Statecraft*, Vo1.17 (2006) p 721.
4. John, Viscount Morley, *Recollections*, 2 vols (Macmillan, London: 1917) I, pp 161–2.
5. Watson, *Georges Clemenceau*, pp 220–1.
6. Watson, *Georges Clemenceau*, pp 224–5.
7. David Robin Watson, 'The making of French foreign policy under the first Clemenceau government, 1906–9', *English Historical Review*, LXXXVI (1971) pp 774–82.
8. A masterly synthesis is provided in David Stevenson, *1914–1918, The History of the First World War* (Allen Lane, London: 2004) pp 3–43, hereafter Stevenson, *1914–1918*.

2: Clemenceau in French Politics

1. Colonel Edward House called him 'The ablest reactionary in Paris', House Diary, 1 April 1919, quoted by Stephen A Shuker in Manfred F Boemeke *et al* (eds), *The Treaty of Versailles, a Reassessment after 75 years* (Cambridge University Press, Cambridge: 1998) p 301.
2. John Maynard Keynes, *The Economic Consequences of the Peace* (Macmillan, London: 1919) pp 28–9.
3. Watson, *Georges Clemenceau*, p 19.
4. Watson, *Georges Clemenceau*, p 21.

5. Watson, *Georges Clemenceau*, pp 53–4.
6. Watson, *Georges Clemenceau*, pp 127–31.
7. Watson, *Georges Clemenceau*, p 149, quoting the report of the trial, *Le Procès Zola*, Vol. 2, p 417.
8. Watson, *Georges Clemenceau*, p 119.
9. David R Watson 'Clemenceau et la Révolution Française', in Jacques Bariéty (ed), *1889: Centénaire de la Révolution Française* (Peter Lang, Berne: 1992).
10. Watson, *Georges Clemenceau*, p 269.
11. Watson, *Georges Clemenceau*, p 271.

3: The End of the War

1. Pierre Renouvin, *The Forms of War Government in France* (Yale University Press, Yale and London: 1927) pp 154–5.
2. Watson, *Georges Clemenceau*, p 278.
3. Albert Thibaudet, *La campagne avec Thucydide* (Plon, Paris: 1922) p 249.
4. Watson, *Georges Clemenceau*, pp 300–4.
5. Watson, *Georges Clemenceau*, p 310.
6. Watson, *Georges Clemenceau*, pp 313–14.
7. Watson, *Georges Clemenceau*, p 326. The best study of the German armistice is P Renouvin, *L'armistice de Rethondes* (Gallimard, Paris: 1968; new ed 2006).
8. Watson, *Georges Clemenceau*, p 335.
9. Clemenceau, *Discours de Guerre*, p 286.
10. Georges Clemenceau, *Discours de Guerre* (Plon, Paris: 1934) pp 285–6.
11. David Lloyd George, *The Truth about the Peace Treaties*, 2 vols (Victor Gollancz, London: 1938) I, p 148.
12. Watson, *Georges Clemenceau*, p 337; J C King, *Foch versus Clemenceau, France and German*

Dismemberment, 1918–1919 (Harvard University Press, Cambridge, Mass: 1960) pp 16–27.
13. Georges Clemenceau, *Discours de Paix* (Plon, Paris: 1938) pp 22–3.

4: Opening of the Conference, January and February

1. General J J H Mordacq, *Le Ministère Clemenceau, Journal d'un témoin* (Plon, Paris: 1930) III, pp 63, 71.
2. Arthur Walworth, *Wilson and his Peacemakers* (W W Norton, New York: 1986) pp 11–12.
3. Marston, *Peace Conference*, p 98.
4. R Poincaré, *Au Service de la France, Neuf Années de Souvenirs* (Plon, Paris: 1974) XI, pp 179–80.
5. R Lansing, *The Big Four* (Hutchinson, London: 1922).
6. Harold Nicolson, *Peacemaking 1919* (Constable, London: 1933) pp 241–2.
7. A J Mayer, *Politics and Diplomacy of Peacemaking, Containment and Counter-revolution at Versailles, 1918–1919* (Weidenfeld and Nicholson, London: 1967); J M Thomson, *Russia, Bolshevism and the Versailles Peace* (1966).

5: The Pause: February to March

1. Lloyd George, *The Truth about the Peace Treaties*, I, p 371.
2. A J Mayer, *Politics and Diplomacy*, pp 456–62; C E Callwell, *Field-Marshal Sir Henry Wilson, His Life and Diaries* (Cassell, London: 1927) II, p 170; C J Lowe and M L Dockrill, *The Mirage of Power* (Routledge and Kegan Paul, London: 1972) II, p 324.
3. Mordacq, *Le Ministère Clemenceau*, III, pp 133–51.

4. George Suarez, *La Vie Orgeilleuse de Clemenceau* (Gallimard, Paris: 1930) p 374.
5. Mordacq, *Le Ministère Clemenceau*, III, p 141.
6. C Seymour (ed), *The Intimate Papers of Colonel House*, 4 vols (E Benn, London: 1928) IV, pp 343–7.
7. Seymour (ed), *The Intimate Papers of Colonel House*, IV, p 345.
8. H I Nelson, *Land and Power: British and Allied Policy on Germany's Frontiers 1916–1919* (Routledge and Kegan Paul, London: 1963) p 165.
9. Poincaré, *Au Service de la France*, XI, pp 244–5.
10. Nelson, *Land and Power*, pp 207–20.
11. Lloyd George, *The Truth about the Peace Treaties*, I, pp 404–12.
12. P Mantoux, *Les Délibérations du Conseil des Quatre*, 2 vols (CNRS, Paris: 1955) I, p 43, hereafter Mantoux, *Délibérations*.
13. Watson, *Georges Clemenceau*, p 348.
14. James F Willis, *Prologue to Nuremberg* (Greenwood Press, Westport and London: 1982) pp 79–81.
15. Willis, *Prologue to Nuremberg*, p 119; John Horne and Alan Kramer, *German Atrocities 1914, a History of Denial* (Yale University Press, New Haven and London: 2000) pp 329–55; Isabel V Hill, *Absolute Destruction, Military Culture and the Practices of War in Imperial Germany* (Cornell University Press, Ithaca and London: 2005) pp 226–62.
16. Horne and Kramer, *German Atrocities 1914*, pp 410–18.

6: The German Frontiers and Treaties of Guarantee

1. Nelson, *Land and Power*, pp 249–81.

2. Watson, *Georges Clemenceau*, pp 337–8, 344–7; King, *Foch Versus Clemenceau*, pp 22–7, 44–72.
3. Watson, *Georges Clemenceau*, p 345.
4. Watson, *Georges Clemenceau*, pp 351–2; Nelson, *Land and Power*, pp 219–46; Robert McCrum, 'French Rhineland policy at the Paris Peace Conference', *Historical Journal*, 21, 3 (1978) pp 623–48; Stephen A Shuker, 'The Rhineland Question', Boemeke *et al* (eds), *The Treaty of Versailles*, pp 275–312.
5. Nelson, *Land and Power*, pp 145–97; Piotr S Wandycz, 'The Polish Question', in Boemeke *et al* (eds), *The Treaty of Versailles*, pp 313–35.

7: Reparations

1. Sally Marks, 'Smoke and Mirrors', in Boemeke *et al* (eds), *The Treaty of Versailles*, pp 330–70; Marc Trachtenberg, *Reparation in World Politics: France and European Economic Diplomacy 1916–1923* (Columbia University Press, New York: 1980), hereafter Trachtenberg, *Reparation*; Bruce Kent, *The Spoils of War: The Politics, Economics and Diplomacy of Reparations, 1918–1932* (Clarendon Press, Oxford: 1989).
2. E Clémentel, *La France et la Politique Economique Interalliée* (Carnegie Economic and Social History of the World War, Presses Universitaire de France, Paris: 1931); George Soutou, 'The French peacemakers', in Boemeke *et al* (eds), *The Treaty of Versailles*, pp 172–82.
3. L L Klotz, *De la Guerre à la Paix* (Payot, Paris: 1924) pp 120–1; R C Self (ed) *The Austen Chamberlain Diary Letters* (Royal Historical Society, Camden Fifth Series, Vol. 5: 1995) p 110.

4. Mantoux, *Délibérations*, I, p 85.
5. A Sharp, *The Versailles Settlement* (Macmillan, London: 1991) p 89.
6. Mantoux, *Délibérations*, I, pp 368–72; Sharp, *The Versailles Settlement*, p 95.
7. Trachtenberg, *Reparation*, pp 66–8.

8: German Signature and the Other Treaties

1. Luckau, *German Delegation*, p 220.
2. Luckau, *German Delegation*, p 225.
3. Mantoux, *Délibérations*, II, pp 253–4.
4. Marston, *Peace Conference*, p 196.
5. Keynes, *Economic Consequences of the Peace*, p 50.
6. Mantoux, *Délibérations*, II, pp 269–73.
7. Mantoux, *Délibérations*, II, pp 408–12.
8. Mordacq, *Le Ministère Clemenceau*, III, p 317.
9. Walworth, *Woodrow Wilson and his Peacemakers*, p 420.
10. A D Low, *The Anschluss Movement 1918–19 and the Paris Peace Conference* (American Philosophical Society, Philadelphia: 1974) p 170.
11. Mantoux, *Délibérations*, I, p 149.
12. Watson, *Georges Clemenceau*, pp 290–2.
13. Sharp, *Versailles Settlement*, pp 169–70.
14. Poincaré, *Au Service de la France*, XI, pp 443–6.
15. Watson, *Georges Clemenceau*, p 371.

9: Defence of the Treaty, July–December 1919

1. Clemenceau, *Discours de Paix*, pp 105–12.
2. Marcel Proust, *Á La Recherche du Temps Perdu, Le Temps Retrouvé* (Bibliothèque de la Pléiade, Gallimard, Paris: 1954) III, p 958.

3. Watson, *Georges Clemenceau*, p 149.
4. R J Young, *Power and Pleasure, Louis Barthou and the Third French Republic* (McGill and Queen's University Press, Montreal and Kingston: 1991) pp 153–60.
5. Clemenceau, *Discours de Paix*, pp 158–63.
6. Clemenceau, *Discours de Paix*, pp 165–222.
7. Keynes, *Economic Consequences of the Peace*, pp 30–3.
8. Clemenceau, *Discours de Paix*, pp 233–81.
9. Watson, *Georges Clemenceau*, pp 385–6.
10. J J H Mordacq, *Clemenceau au soir de sa vie, 1920–1929* (Plon, Paris: 1937) pp 274–5.
11. G Wormser, *La République de Clemenceau* (Presses Universitaires de France, Paris: 1961) p 416.

10: After 1920

1. Mordacq, *Clemenceau au soir de sa vie*, pp 154, 257.
2. Michel Drouin, 'Le voyage de 1922', in Sylvie Brodziak and Michel Drouin (eds), *Clemenceau et le Monde Anglo-saxon* (Geste, La Crèche: 2005) pp 123–45.
3. S I Applebaum, *Clemenceau, Thinker and Writer* (New York: 1948) p 159.
4. Georges Clemenceau, *Grandeurs et Misères d'une Victoire* (Plon, Paris: 1930) pp 333–4, hereafter Clemenceau, *Grandeurs*.
5. Clemenceau, *Grandeurs*, p 346.
6. Clemenceau, *Grandeurs*, p 348.
7. Watson, *Georges Clemenceau*, p 394.
8. Winston Churchill, *Great Contemporaries* (Thornton Butterworth, London: 1937) p 314.
9. Stevenson, *1914–1918*, p 506.

Chronology

YEAR	AGE	THE LIFE AND THE LAND
1841		28 Sep: Born at Mouilleron-en-Pareds, Vendée.
1848	7	Revolution: Second Republic founded.
1851	10	Coup d'état of Napoleon III.
1852	11	Studies at lycée at Nantes. Arrest of his father as republican opponent of Second Empire.
1858	17	Studies medicine at Nantes (to 1861).
1861	20	Studies medicine in Paris (to 1865).
1862	21	23 Feb: Arrested after a republican demonstration.
1863	22	Falls in love with Hortense Kestner, who rejects him. Liberalisation of the Empire begins.
1865	24	Graduates and emigrates to USA.
1869	28	23 Jun: Marries Mary Plummer: returns to France.

YEAR	HISTORY	CULTURE
1841	British sovereignty declared over Hong Kong.	Charles Dickens, ***The Old Curiosity Shop***.
1848	Revolutions in Venice, Berlin, Vienna, Milan and Parma.	'Communist Manifesto' issued by Marx and Engels.
1851	Cuba declares its independence.	Herman Melville, ***Moby Dick***.
1852	South African Republic (Transvaal) established.	Harriet Beecher Stowe, ***Uncle Tom's Cabin***.
1858	Suez Canal Company formed.	Thomas Carlyle, ***Frederick the Great***.
1861	Outbreak of American Civil War.	George Eliot, ***Silas Marner***.
1862	Bismarck becomes Prussian Prime Minister.	Victor Hugo, ***Les Misérables***.
1863	American Civil War: Confederate defeats at Gettysburg and Vicksburg.	Charles Kingsley, ***The Water Babies***.
1865	American Civil War ends.	Lewis Carroll, ***Alice's Adventures in Wonderland***.
1869	Opening of Suez Canal.	Mark Twain, ***The Innocents Abroad***.

YEAR	AGE	THE LIFE AND THE LAND
1870	29	Jun: First child Madeleine, born: followed by Thérese (1872) and Michel (1873). Jul: Franco-Prussian War. Sep: Revolution; Third Republic declared; formation of government of national defence. Siege of Paris (to Jan 1871). 4 Sep: Joins in Revolution and is appointed mayor of Montmartre (18th district of Paris) by new government.
1871	30	28 Jan: Armistice. 8 Feb: Elections for National Assembly – elected deputy for department of Seine (Paris); Thiers becomes 'Head of Executive Power'. 18 Mar: Tries to prevent insurrection that leads to revolutionary Paris Commune. 27 Mar: Resigns as deputy, seeks to mediate between the Commune and the government. 28 May: Commune ends. 23 Jul: Elected municipal councillor for Paris.
1873	32	Thiers resigns; MacMahon becomes President. Germans evacuate last troops from France.
1875	34	Constitutional laws voted.
1876	35	20 Feb: Elected deputy for 18th district of Paris. 'Seize Mai' crisis.
1877	36	24 Oct: Re-elected deputy.
1879	38	MacMahon resigns: Grévy becomes President. Third Republic definitely established.

YEAR	HISTORY	CULTURE
1870	End of Red River Rebellion in Canada. Italians enter Rome and declare it their capital.	Death of Charles Dickens. Jules Verne, ***Twenty Thousand Leagues Under the Sea***.
1871	Britain annexes Kimberley diamond fields in South Africa.	Lewis Carroll, ***Through the Looking Glass***. Charles Darwin, ***The Descent of Man***.
1873	Republic proclaimed in Spain. Famine in Bengal.	Tolstoy, ***Anna Karenina***.
1875	Britain buys Suez Canal shares from Khedive of Egypt.	Mark Twain, ***The Adventures of Tom Sawyer***.
1876	Serbia and Montenegro declare war on Ottoman Empire.	Henry James, ***Roderick Hudson***.
1877	Queen Victoria proclaimed Empress of India. Russo-Turkish War.	Henry James, ***The American***. Rodin, sculpture 'The Age of Bronze'.
1879	Zulu War. Alsace-Lorraine declared an integral part of Germany.	Henry James, ***Daisy Miller***. Tchaikovsky, opera 'Eugen Onegin'.

YEAR	AGE	THE LIFE AND THE LAND
1880	39	***La Justice***, newspaper owned and edited by him, begins publication. France annexes Tahiti.
1881	40	Leads Radical attack on conservative Republicans (Opportunists) led by Gambetta, then by Ferry. Protectorate of Tunisia. Nov: Gambetta becomes prime minister.
1882	41	Opposes Egyptian expedition and colonial policy. Jan: France withdraws from joint Anglo-French expedition to Egypt. Britain establishes informal control of Egypt. Dec: Death of Gambetta.
1883	42	Feb: Ferry becomes prime minister: initiates policy of secular education and colonial expansion in Indo-China.
1885	44	Mar: Brings down Ferry: elected for Paris and Var – chooses Var.
1886	45	Brings Boulanger onto the political scene, then opposes him when he attempts to become a plebiscitary dictator.
1887	46	Defeat of Boulangist movement consolidates the republican regime.
1892	51	Mar: Divorce. Attacked for his relationship with Herz, and tainted by Panama scandal.

YEAR	HISTORY	CULTURE
1880	Transvaal Republic declares independence from Britain.	Dostoevsky, ***The Brothers Karamazov***. Rodin, sculpture The Thinker'.
1881	First Boer War. US President Garfield assassinated. Pogroms against the Jews in Russia.	Henry James, ***Portrait of a Lady***. Offenbach, opera 'Les Contes d'Hoffmann'.
1882	Triple Alliance between Italy, Germany and Austria-Hungary. Hiram Maxim patents his machine gun.	R L Stevenson, ***Treasure Island***. Wagner, opera 'Parsifal'. Tchaikovsky, '1812 Overture'.
1883	British decide to evacuate the Sudan. The Orient Express (Paris-Constantinople) makes its first run.	Death of Wagner. Nietzsche, ***Thus Spake Zarathustra***.
1885	Germany annexes Tanganyika and Zanzibar.	Maupassant, ***Bel Ami***. H Rider Haggard, ***King Solomon's Mines***.
1886	Irish Home Rule Bill introduced by Prime Minister Gladstone. Canadian-Pacific Railway completed.	R L Stevenson, ***Dr Jekyll and Mr Hyde***. Marx's ***Das Kapital*** published in English.
1887	Queen Victoria's Golden Jubilee.	Arthur Conan Doyle, ***A Study in Scarlet***.
1892	Britain and Germany agree on Cameroon.	Bernard Shaw, ***Mrs Warren's Profession***. Tchaikovsky, ballet 'The Nutcracker'.

YEAR	AGE	THE LIFE AND THE LAND
1893	52	Defeated in elections, abandons Parliamentary career;becomes a journalist and man of letters. Franco-Russian alliance signed. Ralliement of Catholics to republic (to 1899).
1894	53	Condemnation of Dreyfus.
1895	54	Publishes several literary works, including a novel ***Les Plus Forts*** (to 1898).
1897	56	Oct: Begins to write for newspaper ***L'Aurore***. Dreyfus affair takes off.
1898	57	Devotes much of his journalism to campaign for Dreyfus, in ***L'Aurore***, ***Le Bloc*** and elsewhere (to 1903). Jan: Publication of ***J'Accuse*** by Zola in ***L'Aurore***.
1899	58	Waldeck-Rousseau forms cabinet. Dreyfus pardoned by presidential decree.
1901	60	Law on Associations used to ban monastic orders and attack Catholic Church.
1902	61	Apr: Elected senator for the Var: returns to forefront of political stage. Combes forms cabinet (to 1905).
1904	63	Entente Cordiale settles British-French colonial differences.

YEAR	HISTORY	CULTURE
1893	Second Irish Home Rule Bill rejected by House of Lords. Benz constructs his four-wheel car.	Oscar Wilde, ***A Woman of No Importance***.
1894	Sino-Japanese War.	G & W Grossmith, ***The Diary of a Nobody***.
1895	Jameson Raid into Transvaal. Marconi invents radio telegraphy	H G Wells, ***The Time Machine***. W B Yeats, ***Poems***.
1897	Queen Victoria's Diamond Jubilee. Zionist Congress in Basel, Switzerland.	H G Wells, ***The Invisible Man***. Edmond Rostand, ***Cyrano de Bergerac***.
1898	Kitchener defeats Mahdists at Omdurman. Spanish-American War. Death of Bismarck.	Thomas Hardy, ***Wessex Poems***. Henry James, ***The Turn of the Screw***. Oscar Wilde, ***The Ballad of Reading Gaol***.
1899	Outbreak of Second Boer War. First Peace Conference at the Hague.	Rudyard Kipling, ***Stalky and Co***. Elgar, 'Enigma Variations'.
1901	Death of Queen Victoria: Edward VII becomes King.	Thomas Mann, ***Die Buddenbrooks.*** Rudyard Kipling, ***Kim.***
1902	Second Boer War ends. Triple Alliance between Austria, Germany and Italy renewed for another six years.	Arthur Conan Doyle, ***The Hound of the Baskervilles***.
1904	Outbreak of Russo-Japanese War.	J M Barrie, ***Peter Pan.***

YEAR	AGE	THE LIFE AND THE LAND
1905	64	Separation of Church and State.
1906	65	Mar: Becomes Minister of Interior in Sarrien cabinet. Social unrest: revolutionary strikes and the revolt of the viticulteurs suppressed. Breach between unified Socialists and other left – wing Republicans – Radical Socialists and Republican Socialists. Oct: Prime Minister – first Clemenceau cabinet. Algeçiras agreement on Morocco.
1909	68	Jul: First government falls. Franco-German agreement on Morocco.
1910	69	Lecture tour of South America.
1912	71	Jan: Overthrows Caillaux cabinet over its colonial agreement with Germany.
1913	72	May: ***L'Homme Libre*** begins publication. Poincaré becomes President of the Republic.
1914	73	Aug: Outbreak of First World War: Sacred Union of all political parties. Oct: ***L'Homme Libre*** renamed ***L'Homme Enchainé*** in protest at censorship. Nov: Briand forms cabinet (to Mar 1917).

YEAR	HISTORY	CULTURE
1905	Russians defeated in Russo-Japanese War.	E M Forster, ***Where Angels Fear to Tread.***
1906	Britain grants self-government to Transvaal and Orange River Colonies. San Francisco earthquake.	John Galsworthy, ***A Man of Property.*** O Henry, ***The Four Million.***
1909	Anglo-German discussions on the control of Baghdad railway.	H G Wells, ***Tono-Bungay***.
1910	King Edward VII dies; succeeded by George V. Liberals win British General Election.	E M Forster, ***Howard's End.***
1912	*Titanic* sinks. First Balkan War. Woodrow Wilson is elected US President.	C G Jung, ***The Theory of Psychoanalysis.***
1913	Second Balkan War. US Federal Reserve System established.	Thomas Mann, ***Death in Venice.***
1914	Archduke Franz Ferdinand of Austria-Hungary and his wife are assassinated in Sarajevo. First World War: Battles of Mons, the Marne and First Ypres; Russians defeated at Battles of Tannenberg and Masurian Lakes.	James Joyce, ***Dubliners.*** Film: Charlie Chaplin in ***Making a Living.***

YEAR	AGE	THE LIFE AND THE LAND
1915	74	Nov: Becomes President of Senate Committees on the Army and of Foreign Affairs.
1916	75	Feb–Dec: Battle of Verdun. Jul–Nov: Battle of the Somme. Dec: Nivelle replaces Joffre as commander-in-chief.
1917	76	Mar: Ribot forms cabinet. May: Failure of Nivelle offensive – mutinies in the French army. Jul: Attacks Malvy for 'defeatism'. Sep: Painlevé replaces Ribot; Unified Socialists withdraw support from government. Oct: Painlevé government defeated in chamber – only cabinet to lose a confidence vote during the war. Nov: Prime Minister: Second Clemenceau government (to Jan 1920).
1918	77	Mar: Meets with British representatives at Doullens to organise resistance to German breakthrough: proposes Foch as supreme Allied commander. German Spring offensives on Western Front fail. Allied summer offensives on Western Front have German army in full retreat. Oct: German appeal to President Wilson. 11 Nov: Armistice. Dec: Visits London.

YEAR	HISTORY	CULTURE
1915	First World War: Battles of Neuve Chappelle and Loos. Gallipoli campaign. *Lusitania* sunk.	John Buchan, *The Thirty-Nine Steps.* Film: *The Birth of a Nation*.
1916	US President Woodrow Wilson is re-elected. Lloyd George becomes British prime minister.	James Joyce, *Portrait of an Artist as a Young Man.* Film: *Intolerance*.
1917	First World War. February Revolution in Russia. USA declares war on Germany. Balfour Declaration favouring the establishment of a national home for the Jewish People in Palestine.	P G Wodehouse, *The Man With Two Left Feet.* T S Eliot, *Prufrock and Other Observations.* Film: *Easy Street*.
1918	First World War. Peace Treaty of Brest-Litovsk between Russia and the Central Powers. Romania signs Peace of Bucharest with Germany and Austria-Hungary. Ex-Tsar Nicholas II and family executed.	Luigi Pirandello, *Six Characters in Search of an Author.*

YEAR	AGE	THE LIFE AND THE LAND
1919	78	18 Jan: President of Peace Conference.
		19 Feb: Injured in assassination attempt.
		13 Mar: End of British support for French franc.
		28 Mar – 28 Jun: Negotiates peace in Council of Four.
		Apr: Withdrawal of French troops from Odessa.
		28 Jun: Treaty of Versailles signed.
		24–25 Sep: Defends Treaty in French Parliament.
		16 Nov: ***Bloc National***, organised to support Clemenceau, wins parliamentary election.
1920	79	16 Jan: Defeated in a preliminary ballot for election of President of the Republic.
		18 Jan: Resigns as prime minister.
		20 Jan: Deschanel elected president – Millerand becomes prime minister.
		4 Feb– 21 Apr: Journey to Egypt.
		Sep: Journey to India and South-East Asia (to May 1921).
		24 Sep: Deschanel resigns as president, replaced by Millerand.
1921	80	Jun: Honorary degree from Oxford University; meeting with Lloyd George.
1922	81	Jan: Poincaré prime minister (to Mar 1924). Nov–Dec: Journey to USA.
1923	82	Occupation of the Ruhr begins.

YEAR	HISTORY	CULTURE
1919	Communist Revolt in Berlin. Benito Mussolini founds fascist movement in Italy. Irish War of Independence begins.	Thomas Hardy, ***Collected Poems.*** George Bernard Shaw, ***Heartbreak House.*** Film: ***The Cabinet of Dr Caligari.***
1920	League of Nations comes into existence. Bolsheviks win Russian Civil War. Government of Ireland Act passed. Adolf Hitler announces his 25-point programme in Munich.	F Scott Fitzgerald, ***This Side of Paradise.*** Franz Kafka, ***The Country Doctor.***
1921	Peace treaty between Russia and Germany. Washington Naval Treaty.	D H Lawrence, ***Women in Love.***
1922	Chanak crisis. League of Nations council approves British mandate in Palestine.	T S Eliot, ***The Waste Land.*** James Joyce, ***Ulysses.***
1923	USSR formally comes into existence. Adolf Hitler's Munich Beer Hall Putsch fails.	P G Wodehouse, ***The Inimitable Jeeves.***

YEAR	AGE	THE LIFE AND THE LAND
1925	84	Jul: End of occupation of the Ruhr. Oct: Locarno treaties.
1926	85	Publishes ***Au Soir de la Pensée***, ***Monet*** and other books: begins to write a defence of the peace settlement (to 1928).
1927	86	French garrison withdrawn from the Saar.
1929	88	24 Nov: Dies in Paris. 26 Nov: Buried with his father in the Vendée.
1930		Posthumous publication of ***Grandeur and Misery of Victory***. Jun: Allies end occupation of Rhineland.
1932		Lausanne conference abandons reparations.
1936		Mar: German reoccupies Rhineland.
1938		German troops enter Austria which is declared part of the German Reich. Munich Agreement hands Sudetenland to Germany.
1939		Germans troops enter Prague. Nazi-Soviet Pact. Sep: German invasion of Poland: Britain and France declare war.

YEAR	HISTORY	CULTURE
1925	Pound Sterling returns to the Gold Standard. Hindenburg, elected President of Germany.	Virginia Woolf, ***Mrs Dalloway.*** Film: ***Battleship Potemkin***.
1926	General Strike in Great Britain. Germany admitted into the League of Nations.	A A Milne, ***Winnie the Pooh.*** Ernest Hemingway, ***The Sun Also Rises.***
1927	Inter-Allied military control of Germany ends.	Virginia Woolf, ***To the Lighthouse.*** Film: ***The Jazz Singer***.
1929	Germany accepts Young Plan at Reparations Conference.	Erich Remarque, ***All Quiet on the Western Front.***
1930	London Naval Treaty. Nazi party in Germany gains 107 seats in Reichstag.	W H Auden, ***Poems.*** Noel Coward, ***Private Lives.***
1932	F D Roosevelt wins US Presidential election.	Aldous Huxley, ***Brave New World.***
1936	Outbreak of Spanish Civil War. British end protectorate over Egypt.	J M Keynes, ***General Theory of Employment, Interest***.
1938	Japanese puppet government of China at Nanjing.	Graham Greene, ***Brighton Rock.*** Film: ***The Adventures of Robin Hood.***
1939	Italy invades Albania. Spanish Civil War ends. Japanese-Soviet clashes in Manchuria. Soviets invade Finland.	John Steinbeck, ***The Grapes of Wrath***. Film: ***Gone with the Wind***.

Further Reading

Like most French politicians of the Third Republic Clemenceau did not leave behind him a collection of private papers on the scale that was normal in Britain at that time. He did not keep copies of letters he wrote, and retained very few of the letters he received. However, after his death, the modest Paris apartment in which he had lived for nearly 40 years was preserved as a museum, with another apartment on the next floor as an annexe containing material for the documentation of his life. Among other material this museum gradually acquired from their recipients letters or copies of letters written by him. These sources can now be consulted in the manuscript department of the National Library of France, and an edition of Clemenceau's letters is about to be published.

Some of the documentary material in the museum has been published in Georges Wormser, *La République de Clemenceau* (Presses Universitaires de France, Paris: 1961), and *Clemenceau vu de près* (Hachette, Paris: 1979). His speeches of this period can be found in *Discours de Guerre* (Plon, Paris: 1934) and *Discours de Paix* (Plon, Paris: 1938). Clemenceau did not write his memoirs, being very different in this respect from Winston Churchill who sought to control the verdict of history by writing it himself. *Grandeur and Misery of Victory*, on which Clemenceau was working during his last months and left unfinished, does not amount to memoirs, but consists of a rebuttal of the arguments of Foch and Poincaré against his conduct of the peace negotiation. However, some equivalent of autobiographical fragments can be found in the books published by his private secretary, Jean Martet, *M Clemenceau peint par lui-même* (1929), *Le Silence de M Clemenceau* (1929), and *Le Tigre* (1930). An English version entitled *Clemenceau, the events of his life as told by himself* (Longmans, London: 1930) exists. Martet took detailed notes, and his account of Clemenceau's reminiscences can be regarded as reliable: he also printed a certain amount of documentation, mainly concerned with Clemenceau's early life. The six detailed volumes by his military *chef de cabinet* General J J H Mordacq, *Le Ministère Clemenceau, Journal d'un témoin*, 4 vols, (Plon, Paris: 1930–1), and *Clemenceau, au soir de sa vie, 1920–29* (Plon, Paris: 1933) are almost a primary source. Other books purporting to reproduce reminiscences are much less reliable.

There are few good biographies of Clemenceau in English. Three worth consulting are G Bruun, *Clemenceau* (Harvard: 1943), David Robin Watson, *Clemenceau, a political biography* (Eyre Methuen, London: 1974), and David S Newhall, *Clemenceau, a Life at War* (Edward Mellen Press, Lampeter: 1991). Churchill's essay on Clemenceau in *Great Contemporaries* (Thornton Butterworth, London: 1937) is worth reading. The character sketch in J M Keynes, *The Economic Consequences of the Peace* (Macmillan, London: 1919) should be read; however wrong, Keynes' view of Clemenceau has had immense influence.

In French by far the best and most authoritative biography is that of Jean-Baptiste Duroselle, *Clemenceau* (Fayard, Paris: 1988). Much valuable material is to be found in the proceedings of two conferences, 1979 for the centenary of Clemenceau's death, and 2004 for the centenary of the Anglo-French entente: *Clemenceau et la justice* (Publications de la Sorbonne, Paris: 1983), Sylvie Brodziak and Michel Drouin (eds), *Georges Clemenceau et le Monde Anglo-saxon* (Geste, La Crèche: 2005). There have been several recent biographical essays by eminent historians. These include P Miquel, *Clemenceau, la guerre et la paix* (Tallandier, Paris: 1996) covering the years 1917 to 1920, Jean-Noel Jeanneney, *Clemenceau portrait d'un homme libre* (Mengès, Paris: 2005) with many illustrations, Michel Winock, *Clemenceau* (Perrin, Paris: 2007) and Pierre Guiral, *Clemenceau en son temps* (Grasset, Paris: 1994). The best of the older biographies in French are Gustave Geffroy, *Clemenceau, sa vie, son oeuvre* (Larousse, Paris: 1919) and Georges Michon, *Clemenceau* (M Rivière, Paris: 1931). An important book on French government in wartime is Pierre Renouvin, *The forms of war government in France* (Yale University Press, New Haven: 1927).

The general background to the peace settlement is illuminated by the following works on French foreign policy over the last century and a half: David R Watson, 'France, Europe and the world: international politics since 1880,' in James McMillan (ed), *Modern France, Short Oxford History of France* (Oxford University Press, Oxford: 2003), J F V Keiger, *France and the World since 1870* (Arnold, London: 2001), P M H Bell, *France and Britain 1900–1940, entente and estrangement* (Longman, London: 1996), Robert and Isabelle Tombs, *That Sweet Enemy: The French and the British from the Sun King to the Present* (Heinemann, London: 2006) Chapters 9–12.

Not confined to France, but the essential synthesis on the history of international relations of this period, Zara Steiner, *The Lights that Failed, European International History, 1919–1933* (Oxford University Press, Oxford: 2005).

A bibliography of the peace negotiations would be immense. Primary sources include the key debates of the Council of Four, Paul Mantoux, *Les Délibérations du Conseil des Quatre, 24 mars-28 juin 1919* (Centre National de la Recherche Scientifique, Paris: 1955), translated into English as P Mantoux, *The Deliberations of the Council of Four, Notes of the official interpreter*, translated and edited by A S Link (Princeton: 1992) and the minutes of the Council of Ten and of much other documentation have been printed in *Foreign Relations of the United States, Paris Peace Conference 1919* (Washington) 13 vols.

Documents on British Foreign Policy 1919–1939 (HMSO, London: 1947) begin after the signing of the Treaty of Versailles, on 1 July 1919. The proceedings of the Supreme Council (Heads of Delegations) which continued the work of the Council of Ten and Council of Four after that date, are available in the first volumes of the first Series. Publication of French documents for this period has begun but has not yet reached 1919: *Documents Diplomatiques Français, 1914–1919*, ed J C Montant, and *1920–32*, ed J Bariéty (Imprimerie Nationale: Paris, and Peter Lang, Berne: 2003 seq). However, some French documentary material was printed in A Tardieu, *La Paix* (Paris: 1921) translated as *The Truth about the Treaty* (London: 1921) and in Mermeix (ed), *Le Combat des trois, Notes et documents sur la conférence de la paix* (Ollendorff, Paris: 1922).

Another essential primary source is the diary of the President of the Republic, available in the MSS department of the

National Library, and now printed as a supplementary volume to his memoirs: Raymond Poincaré, *Au service de la France, Vol XI, A la Recherche de la Paix, 1919* (Plon, Paris: 1974). Other primary source material is in Louis Loucheur, *Carnets secrets 1908–1932*, ed Jacques de Launay (Brepils, Bruxelles: 1967), and L L Klotz, *De la guerre à la Paix, Souvenirs et documents* (Payot, Paris: 1924). Discussion of the treaty in the French Parliament is recorded in the *Journal Officiel*; it is also in E Beau de Lomenie, *Le Débat de Ratification du Traité de Versailles* (Denoel, Paris: 1945).

General books on the peace settlement which are essential for assessment of French policy include: Paul Birdsall, *Versailles, Twenty Years After* (Allen and Unwin, London: 1941), Manfred F Boemeke, Gerald D Feldman and Elisabeth Glaser (eds), *The Treaty of Versailles, a Reassessment after 75 years* (Cambridge University Press, Cambridge: 1998), H Elcock, *Portrait of a Decision, the Council of Four and the Treaty of Versailles* (Eyre Methuen, London: 1972), and Margaret Macmillan, *Peacemakers, the Paris Peace Conference of 1919 and its attempt to end War* (John Murray, London: 2001). The best short study is by Alan Sharp, *The Versailles Settlement, peacemaking in Paris 1919* (Macmillan, London: 1991). Others are Michael Dockrill, and John Fisher (eds), *The Paris Peace Conference, 1919, Peace without Victory?* (Palgrave: 2001), and Michael Dockrill and J D Goold, *Peace without Promise: Britain and the Peace Conferences 1919–23* (Batsford, London: 1981). There is a short essay by D R Watson, 'The making of the Treaty of Versailles', in Neville Waites (ed) *Troubled Neighbours: Franco-British relations in the Twentieth Century* (Weidenfeld and Nicolson, London: 1971). G S Noble, *Policies and Opinions at Paris* (New York: 1935) has now been superseded by Pierre Miquel, *La Paix de Versailles et l'Opinion Publique Française* (Flammarion, Paris: 1972). C Carlier and G H Soutou (eds), *1918–1925, Comment faire la paix?* (Economica, Paris: 2001). Jacques Bariéty, *Les Relations Franco-Allemands après la Premiere Guerre Mondiale 10 Nov 1918–10 jan 1925* (Pedone, Paris: 1977). Pierre Renouvin, *11 Novembre 1918, L'Armistice de Rethondes* (Gallimard, Paris: 1968), *Le Traité de Versailles* (Flammarion, Questions d'histoire, Paris: 1969). David Stevenson, *1914–1918 The History of the First World War* (Allen Lane, London: 2004) *Part 4, Legacy,* and *The First World War and International Politics* (Oxford University Press, Oxford: 1988) Chapter 6, also *French War Aims against Germany 1914–1919* (Clarendon Press, Oxford: 1982), Chapters V–VII.

Books on particular topics

On the Rhineland and the treaties of guarantee: H I Nelson, *Land and Power, British and Allied Policy on Germany's Frontiers 1916–1919* (Routledge, London: 1963), A Lentin, 'Lloyd George, Clemenceau and the elusive Anglo-French guarantee treaty', in Alan Sharp and Glyn Stone (eds), *Anglo-French relations in the Twentieth Century* (Routledge, London: 2000), David Stevenson, 'France at the Paris Peace Conference, addressing the dilemmas of security', in Robert Boyce (ed), *French Foreign and Defence Policy 1918–1940, The Decline and Fall of a Great Power* (Routledge, London: 1998), Sally Marks, 'Mésentente cordiale: the Anglo-French relationship 1921–1922', and William R Keylor, 'France's futile quest for American military protection 1919–1922', both in Marta Petricioli (ed), *A Missed Opportunity: 1922 The Reconstruction of Europe* (Peter Lang, Bern: 1995). W A McDougall, *France's Rhineland diplomacy 1914–1924; the last bid for a balance of power in Europe* (Princeton: 1978).

R McCrum, 'French Rhineland policy at the Paris Peace Conference 1919', *Historical Journal*, 21, 3 (1978) pp 623–48.

On the Polish frontiers: P S Wandycz, *France and her Eastern Allies 1919–25* (Minneapolis: 1962).

On reparations and war debts: S D Carls, *Louis Loucheur and the shaping of modern France* (Baton Rouge: 1993), Dan P Silverman, *Reconstructing Europe after the Great War* (Harvard University Press, Cambridge, Mass: 1982); also, as well as the vast older literature, Bruce Kent, *The Spoils of War, The Politics, Economics and Diplomacy of Reparations 1918–1932* (Clarendon Press, Oxford: 1989), Arthur Turner, *The Cost of the War, British Policy on French War Debts, 1918–1932* (Sussex Academic Press, Brighton: 1998), Denise Artaud, *La Question des dettes interalliées et la reconstruction de l'Europe, 1917–1929* (Atelier des théses, Lille and Paris: 1978), M Trachtenberg, *Reparation in World Politics, France and European Economic Diplomacy 1916–1923* (Columbia University Press, New York: 1980).

On the Middle East: Christopher Andrew and A S Kanya-Forstner, *France Overseas: the Great War and the Climax of French Overseas Expansion* (Thames & Hudson, London: 1981).

On atrocities and war crimes: James F Willis, *Prologue to Nuremberg, the politics and diplomacy of punishing war criminals* (Greenwood Press, Westport and London: 1982).

Picture Sources

The author and publishers wish to express their thanks to the following sources of illustrative material and/or permission to reproduce it. They will make proper acknowledgements in future editions in the event that any omissions have occurred.

Topham Picturepoint: pp vi, xiv, 64, 162.

Endpapers

The Signing of Peace in the Hall of Mirrors, Versailles, 28th June 1919 by Sir William Orpen (Bridgeman Art Library)
Front row: Dr Johannes Bell (Germany) signing with Herr Hermann Müller leaning over him
Middle row (seated, left to right): General Tasker H Bliss, Col E M House, Mr Henry White, Mr Robert Lansing, President Woodrow Wilson (United States); M Georges Clemenceau (France); Mr David Lloyd George, Mr Andrew Bonar Law, Mr Arthur J Balfour, Viscount Milner, Mr G N Barnes (Great Britain); Prince Saionji (Japan)
Back row (left to right): M Eleftherios Venizelos (Greece); Dr Afonso Costa (Portugal); Lord Riddell (British Press); Sir George E Foster (Canada); M Nikola Pašić (Serbia);

M Stephen Pichon (France); Col Sir Maurice Hankey, Mr Edwin S Montagu (Great Britain); the Maharajah of Bikaner (India); Signor Vittorio Emanuele Orlando (Italy); M Paul Hymans (Belgium); General Louis Botha (South Africa); Mr W M Hughes (Australia)

Jacket Images

(Front): akg Images.
(Back): *Peace Conference at the Quai d'Orsay* by Sir William Orpen (akg Images).
Left to right (seated): Signor Orlando (Italy); Mr Robert Lansing, President Woodrow Wilson (United States); M Georges Clemenceau (France); Mr David Lloyd George, Mr Andrew Bonar Law, Mr Arthur J Balfour (Great Britain); Left to right (standing): M Paul Hymans (Belgium); Mr Eleftherios Venizelos (Greece); The Emir Feisal (The Hashemite Kingdom); Mr W F Massey (New Zealand); General Jan Smuts (South Africa); Col E M House (United States); General Louis Botha (South Africa); Prince Saionji (Japan); Mr W M Hughes (Australia); Sir Robert Borden (Canada); Mr G N Barnes (Great Britain); M Ignacy Paderewski (Poland)

Index

V

W

Y

Z

UK PUBLICATION: November 2008 to December 2010
CLASSIFICATION: Biography/History/
International Relations
FORMAT: 198 × 128mm
EXTENT: 208pp
ILLUSTRATIONS: 6 photographs plus 4 maps
TERRITORY: world

Chronology of life in context, full index, bibliography innovative layout with sidebars

Woodrow Wilson: United States of America by Brian Morton
Friedrich Ebert: Germany by Harry Harmer
Georges Clemenceau: France by David Watson
David Lloyd George: Great Britain by Alan Sharp
Prince Saionji: Japan by Jonathan Clements
Wellington Koo: China by Jonathan Clements
Eleftherios Venizelos: Greece by Andrew Dalby
From the Sultan to Atatürk: Turkey by Andrew Mango
The Hashemites: The Dream of Arabia by Robert McNamara
Chaim Weizmann: The Dream of Zion by Tom Fraser
Piip, Meierovics & Voldemaras: Estonia, Latvia & Lithuania by Charlotte Alston
Ignacy Paderewski: Poland by Anita Prazmowska
Beneš, Masaryk: Czechoslovakia by Peter Neville
Károlyi & Bethlen: Hungary by Bryan Cartledge
Karl Renner: Austria by Jamie Bulloch
Vittorio Orlando: Italy by Spencer Di Scala
Paśić & Trumbić: The Kingdom of Serbs, Croats and Slovenes by Dejan Djokic
Aleksandŭr Stamboliĭski: Bulgaria by R J Crampton
Ion Bratianu: Romania by Keith Hitchin
Paul Hymans: Belgium by Sally Marks
General Smuts: South Africa by Antony Lentin
William Hughes: Australia by Carl Bridge
William Massey: New Zealand by James Watson
Sir Robert Borden: Canada by Martin Thornton
Maharajah of Bikaner: India by Hugh Purcell
Afonso Costa: Portugal by Filipe Ribeiro de Meneses
Epitácio Pessoa: Brazil by Michael Streeter
South America by Michael Streeter
Central America by Michael Streeter
South East Asia by Andrew Dalby
The League of Nations by Ruth Henig
Consequences of Peace: The Versailles Settlement – Aftermath and Legacy by Alan Sharp